AnimalWays

Deer

AnimalWays

Deer

Rebecca Stefoff

Marshall Cavendish
Benchmark
New York

With thanks to Jody Enck, Department of Natural Resources, Cornell University, for his expert reading of this manuscript.

Marshall Cavendish Benchmark
99 White Plains Road
Tarrytown, NY 10591-9001
www.marshallcavendish.us

Library of Congress Cataloging-in-Publication Data

Stefoff, Rebecca,
Deer/ Rebecca Stefoff.
p. cm.—(Animalways)
Summary: "A summary of the life cycle, diet, behavior, anatomy, and conservation status of deer"—Provided by publisher.
Includes bibliographical references and index
ISBN 978-0-7614-2534-2
1.Deer—Juvenile literature. I. Title
QL737.U55S745 2007
599.65—dc22
2007016932

Publisher: Michelle Bisson
Art Director: Anahid Hamparian

Photo research by Candlepants Incorporated

Cover Photo: *Minden Pictures/Tui De Roy*

The photographs in this book are used by permission and through the courtesy of:
Corbis: Raymond Gehman, 2, back cover; Archivo Iconografico, S.A., 31; Christophe Loviny, 37; Jason Hosking/zefa, 47; Michael Clark; Frank Lane Picture Agency, 56; Robert Y. Ono, 58; Hamid Sardar, 61; Erwin Patzelt/dpa, 66; George D. Lepp, 75; Yann Arthus-Bertrand, 78. *Minden Pictures:* Tim Fitzharris, 9; Patrico Robles GIL/Sierra Madre, 16; Thomas Mangelsen, 59; Mark Raycroft, 62; Claus Meyer, 64; SA Team/Foto Natura, 65; Tui De Roy, 69; Michael Quinton, 81; Jim Brandenburg, 85; Michael Durham, 91. *Super Stock:* age fotostock, 13. *Peter Arnold Inc.:* S.E. Arndt, 14; Neil McIntyre/WWI, 23; J. Mallwitz, 25; M. Blachas, 26; M. Lane, 44; A. Rouse, 45; S. Muller, 49; Roland Seitre, 50; Sylvain Cordier, 51; Klein, 52; J. Giustina, 54; Steve Kaufman, 63; *The Image Works:* Fortean/Topham, 34; ArenaPal/Topham, 88. *Photo Researchers Inc.:* Mandal/Ranjit, 41; William H. Mullins, 74.

Printed in Malaysia
3 5 6 4 2

Contents

Animal Kingdom

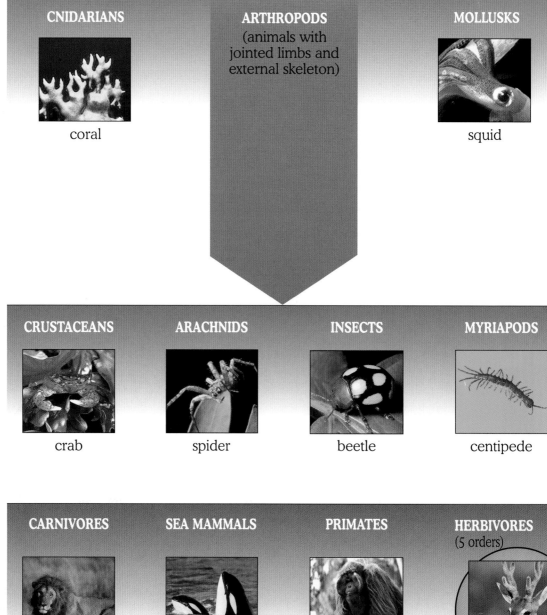

CNIDARIANS

coral

ARTHROPODS
(animals with jointed limbs and external skeleton)

MOLLUSKS

squid

CRUSTACEANS

crab

ARACHNIDS

spider

INSECTS

beetle

MYRIAPODS

centipede

CARNIVORES

lion

SEA MAMMALS

whale

PRIMATES

orangutan

HERBIVORES
(5 orders)

DEER

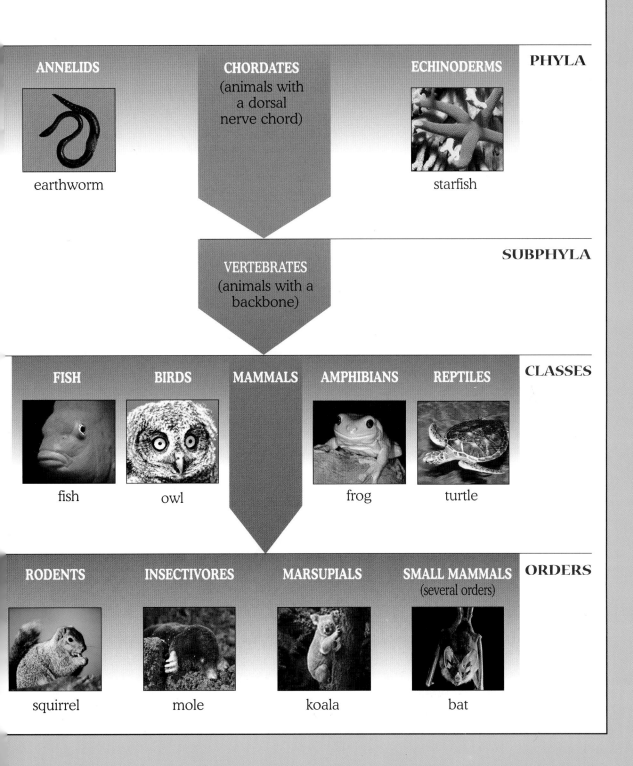

PHYLA

ANNELIDS

earthworm

CHORDATES
(animals with
a dorsal
nerve chord)

ECHINODERMS

starfish

SUBPHYLA

VERTEBRATES
(animals with a
backbone)

CLASSES

FISH

fish

BIRDS

owl

MAMMALS

AMPHIBIANS

frog

REPTILES

turtle

ORDERS

RODENTS

squirrel

INSECTIVORES

mole

MARSUPIALS

koala

SMALL MAMMALS
(several orders)

bat

1 Meet the Cervids

In autumn the rolling slopes of eastern Oregon's Blue Mountains are a patchwork of green and gold. Tracts of pine and fir trees blanket the slopes, broken by sun-parched meadows and valleys. As night falls over the woodlands and grasslands, an eerie sound shatters the silence. A loud, low bellow rises to an earsplitting shriek, then descends again. Half a dozen deep grunts follow. Suddenly the same penetrating sound explodes from another direction, even louder.

The cry ringing out over the shadowy valleys is called bugling, because it sounds like the blare of a brass bugle. It is made by bull elk, male animals that can stand nearly 5 feet (1.5 meters) high at the shoulder and weigh as much as 770 pounds (340 kilograms). The bulls are bugling to advertise their strength. The elk mating season is starting, and a bull's cry serves two purposes. It lures females, and it also communicates a warning or challenge to rival males. As mating season advances, the challenge can become physical. The two bulls that are now bugling at one another through the night may soon lock antlers in a desperate shoving match.

LARGE, SPREADING ANTLERS SHOW THAT THIS AMERICAN ELK, OR WAPITI, IS A MATURE MALE. DURING MATING SEASON HE WILL CHALLENGE OTHER BULLS—OR DEFEND HIS FEMALES FROM CHALLENGERS.

On the other side of the world, dense tropical forest clings to a steep hillside in northeastern Myanmar, formerly known as Burma. As rain drips down through the canopy onto the forest floor, a glossy green fern slowly parts, and a gray-brown head pokes through. After a cautious look around, a small creature steps out and picks its way to the edge of a stream. Standing 2 feet (0.6 meters) high at the shoulder, weighing 25 pounds (11 kilograms), it is a leaf muntjac. Suddenly its ears stand upright—it has heard something. With a call of alarm that sounds just like the barking of a dog, the muntjac slips behind the fern and disappears.

The leaf muntjac is one of the world's least-known mammals, and possibly one of its rarest, while the elk—also called wapiti—is fairly common in parts of the western regions of Canada and the United States. Although the mighty elk is as different in size from the leaf muntjac as a horse is from a large rabbit, the elk and the muntjac are close relatives. Both of them belong to a group that biologists call the Cervidae, the larger of the two families of deer. Deer are often called cervids because of this scientific name.

Deer are found on every continent except Antarctica, although Africa has only one native species, and Australia's deer were brought there in recent times by humans. More than fifty species of deer exist today, from the familiar white-tailed and mule deer of the United States to northern Scandinavia's reindeer herds and the small, shy forest deer of Asia and South America. Though cervids show great variety in appearance and habits, they also share many features that are legacies of their common heritage. Evolution has shaped deer for life as alert, fast-moving grazers and browsers on vegetation.

Deer are herbivores, or animals that eat only plant matter. (Deer eat some insects, too, but only because the insects happen to be on the plant matter.) Their biology has been shaped by two main challenges. One challenge is escaping from predators, the carnivores or meat-eaters who prey on herbivores. The other challenge is living on plant materials that are often low in nutrition and hard to digest, such as grasses, leaves, and twigs. In their physical structure, their ways of moving, and their senses, deer are well adapted to meet these challenges.

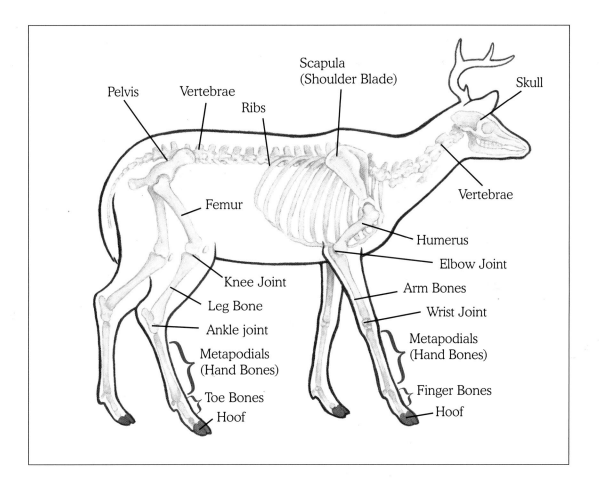

THE SKELETON OF A WHITE-TAILED DEER SHOWS HOW SIMILAR CERVIDS ARE TO OTHER MAMMALS IN THEIR GENERAL SKELETAL STRUCTURE. THE BONES OF THE DEER'S LEGS AND FEET, FOR EXAMPLE, ARE MODIFICATIONS OF THE SAME BONES FOUND IN THE LEGS (AND ARMS) OF OTHER MAMMALS, FROM WHALES TO HUMANS.

A Specialized Skeleton

A deer's anatomy, or physical structure, reflects its way of life. Deer are four-legged animals. Their necks are long, so that a standing deer can reach grass or other vegetation on the ground. Their legs are long, too, with large muscles for fast, powerful movement. Scientists call deer cursorial animals, which means that they are physically adapted for running.

Like horses, antelope, and some other fast-moving herbivores, deer are ungulates, or hoofed mammals. Each leg ends in hooves that are expanded toenails. Hooves are made of keratin, a protein that takes the form of braided filaments, or strands, of cells. Keratin is the substance from which other animals' claws, and human fingernails and toenails, are made. A deer's hooves are far stronger than a person's nails, however, because in hooves the keratin occurs in many thick sheets, reinforced by fibers of the same material running in all directions. The result is a hard, durable substance that is tougher and more crack-resistant than bone. It is strong enough to support the full weight of the animal, even when the deer is running or jumping with force.

The name *ungulate* comes from the unguis, the tough outer plate of a hoof or toenail. An ungulate is any animal that walks on its unguis. When an ungulate takes a step, its hooves, not its feet or even its digits, make contact with the ground. (In some species, the digits may also touch the ground behind the front edge of the hoof, but it is the unguis that makes the main contact.)

Why would deer evolve to walk on the tips of their toenails? For speed. Researchers in biomechanics, the science of how organisms' bodies move, have learned that when the area that touches the ground with each stride is reduced, an animal takes a longer stride, and therefore covers more ground in the same amount of time. When deer move, only their toetips, the smallest

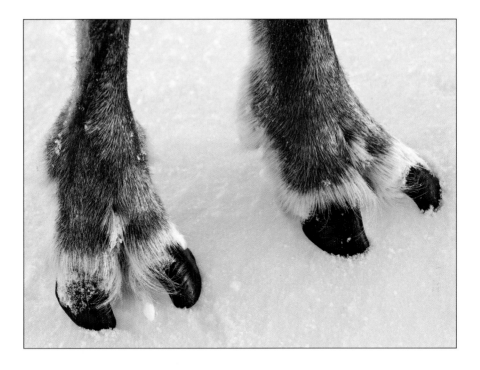

THE REINDEER'S HOOVES ARE SPREAD WIDE, GIVING THE ANIMAL A BROAD WALKING SURFACE ON EACH FOOT. THE HOOVES ACT LIKE SNOWSHOES, HELPING THE ANIMAL TRAVEL ACROSS SNOW WITHOUT SINKING DEEPLY INTO IT.

possible area, touch the ground. This gives each species of deer the longest possible stride for its size, which helps the animals move fast.

Deer have four toes on each foot. The middle two toes, which correspond to the middle and ring fingers on a human hand, touch the ground and have fully developed hooves. These are the hooves on which the deer walks. The outer toes correspond to the human index finger and little fingers. On a deer, these toes are much smaller than the middle toes, and they do not touch the ground. Called dewclaws, they appear on the backs' of deers' lower legs, just above the hooves.

A DEER WALKS ON ITS TWO CENTER TOES. JUST ABOVE THEM ARE THE TWO SMALLER OUTER TOES, CALLED DEWCLAWS.

What we think of as a deer's leg is really its leg plus part of its foot. The metapodials—bones that in humans are found in the palms of the hands and the soles of the feet—have become lengthened in deer. They form the lower parts of deers' legs. The deer's upper leg bones—the femur in the rear legs and the humerus in the forelegs—are short but thick. They are able to anchor the large masses of muscle needed to propel deer forward at high speed, or to push them into bounding leaps.

The legs and feet of a deer's skeleton are well adapted to rapid movement. The American moose and elk, among the largest members of the deer family, can reach speeds of 45 miles (72 kilometers) per hour over distances of about half a mile (800 meters). The white-tailed deer can reach similar speeds, but it can keep them up only for an eighth of a mile (200 meters) or so. The caribou, or reindeer, gallops at about 35 miles (56 kilometers) per hour, which is also the top speed of the mule deer.

Deer have a variety of gaits, or ways of moving, depending on the species and the conditions. They walk by moving opposing pairs of legs at the same time—in other words, the deer steps forward with the left foreleg and the right rear leg and then, after they are planted, with the right foreleg and the left rear leg. The legs move in the same way, but faster, when the deer is trotting, a gait that is slower than running but demands less energy. For some large species, trotting is an efficient way to cover long distances. Caribou, for example, can trot at an average speed of 8 miles (14 kilometers) per hour, in a smooth, fluid motion, for half a day or longer.

Running is highly varied. Some large species, such as moose, caribou, and elk, run with a heavy, pounding gallop. A number of other species, such as mule deer and the much smaller musk deer, have a springing type of run, leaping forward with powerful thrusts from the large muscles of their hind legs. This type of bounding or leaping gallop is called saltatorial running.

Some deer species have an even more energetic gait known as stotting (also called pronking). Stotting is a springy motion that looks a bit like bouncing on four pogo sticks. When a deer stots, all four of its hooves leave the ground at once, then touch down and push off again, and the deer moves forward in great bounds. Stotting is a good way to startle and perhaps discourage an intruder, to climb a steep hillside, or to outrun a predator with a burst of speed. The mule deer of the American West are noted for their stiff-legged stotting, which can carry them up the steep walls of canyons. No deer stots all the time, however, or for long periods of time, because it requires too much energy.

AS THEY FORAGE AMONG YUCCA PLANTS IN THE DESERT OF NORTHERN MEXICO, A FEMALE MULE DEER AND HER FAWN ARE ALERT FOR SIGNS OF DANGER. IF THREATENED, THEY CAN BOUND UP STEEP SLOPES TO ESCAPE.

Stotting is not the same thing as jumping. Although deer of some species stot their way over obstacles, others simply jump across streams or over fences. When a deer jumps, its front hooves leave the ground first, and it pushes off with its hind legs. Many species are good jumpers. White-tailed deer, for example, have been known to clear fences as high as 9.5 feet (3 meters), as many homeowners have discovered upon waking to find deer swimming in their fenced-in pools. Deer have also been recorded jumping horizontal distances of 29 feet (8.7 meters).

Just as a cervid's hooves and legs are well-suited to a cursorial life, its tongue and teeth are adapted to a vegetarian diet. Deer have long, flexible tongues that they use for pulling plants

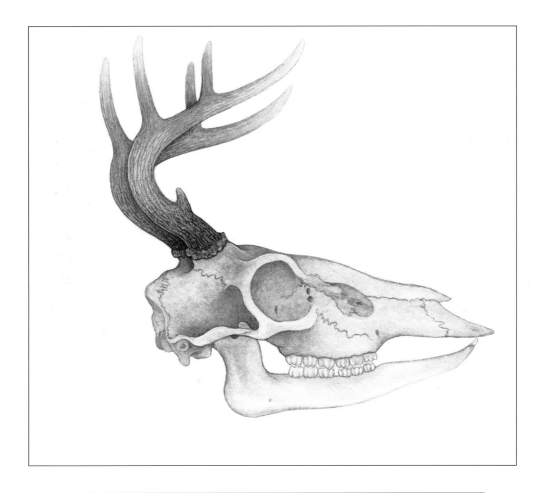

THIS DEER'S SKULL SHOWS THE SHARP, CHISELLIKE CUTTING TEETH AT THE VERY FRONT OF THE LOWER JAW, AND THE BROAD, FLAT CHEWING TEETH ALONG THE SIDE. THE ORBITS, OR EYE OPENINGS, ARE BIG ENOUGH TO HOLD THE DEER'S RELATIVELY LARGE EYEBALLS.

into their mouths. They have thirty-two or thirty-four teeth, depending on the species, divided into front and side groups. The lower front teeth form a row across the front of the deer's jaw. They are narrow, chisel-shaped, and sharp, useful for plucking grass or leaves and biting through tough stems. Deer have no upper front teeth. Instead they have a hard, bony pad for the lower teeth to bite against. Some species, though, have one upper tooth—a canine tooth, the longest and sharpest of the biting teeth—on each side. In a few species, such as Chinese water deer and musk deer, these upper canines are long enough to be visible as short, sharp tusks.

A deer's side teeth are sometimes called cheek teeth because they are located far back in the mouth, inside the cheeks. There are twelve molars on each side, six in the upper jaw and six in the lower jaw. These are broad, flat-topped teeth suitable for grinding and chewing. Vegetation contains varying amounts of a tough material called cellulose, which makes up the walls of plant cells. Animals that eat plants must masticate, or chew, their food thoroughly to break down the cellulose. Like other herbivores, deer need numerous strong molars for this task of serious mastication. They also require a digestive system that can get adequate nutrition from a high volume of plant matter.

High-Powered Digestion

Deer are ruminants, or cud-chewers. The ruminants are herbivores that have complex multipart stomachs. Their process of digestion involves regurgitating and rechewing their food, helped along by microscopic organisms, such as bacteria and yeasts.

A large percentage of the nutrients in many plants is contained in the walls of the cells, not inside the cells themselves.

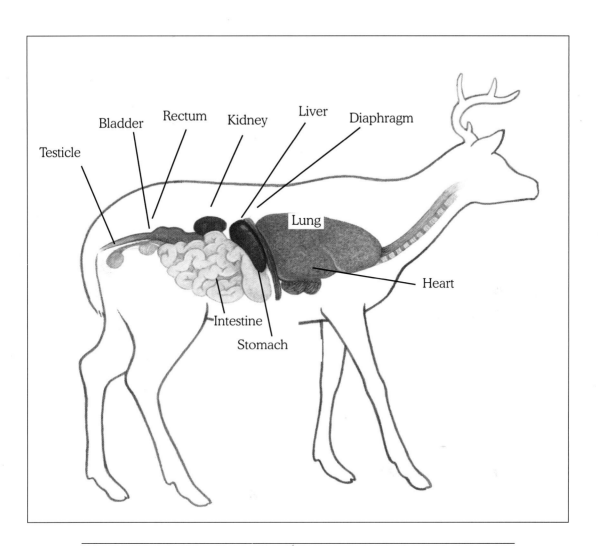

Testicle · Bladder · Rectum · Kidney · Liver · Diaphragm · Lung · Heart · Intestine · Stomach

THE INTERNAL ORGANS OF DEER ARE NOT SO DIFFERENT FROM OUR OWN.

Getting that energy requires digesting the cellulose, or breaking it down and turning it into carbohydrates that can be absorbed by the body. This is done with biological chemicals called cellulytic enzymes, in a process called fermentation. Mammals don't produce cellulytic enzymes, but microorganisms do. Ruminants' stomachs contain billions of these microorganisms.

A deer's stomach has four chambers, or parts. When a deer eats, the food passes down the esophagus and into the first chamber of the stomach, the rumen. The rumen is the largest part of the stomach. It contains microorganisms that mix with the food and start breaking down the cellulose. The rumen also acts as a storage chamber for food. The deer periodically regurgitates a wad of food from the rumen into the mouth and chews it for a second, third, or fourth time.

The mastication of regurgitated plant food is called chewing the cud, and it has several advantages. First, it lets the deer consume a lot of food as quickly as possible, without having to chew each bite of food thoroughly. This minimizes the amount of time that the deer must spend eating with its head down, vulnerable to predators. Later, when the deer is resting and can remain highly alert for predators, it can chew the food at its leisure. Second, cud-chewing breaks the food into smaller and smaller pieces, while mixing it more and more thoroughly with the microorganisms that are starting the digestive process.

When food has been well chewed and is broken down into small particles, it passes into the second chamber of the stomach, the reticulum. Digestion of the cellulose continues in the reticulum, which is basically a fermentation vat. Food usually remains in the reticulum longer than in any other chamber. Eventually the mixture of microorganisms, broken-down cellulose, and nutrients moves on to the third chamber, the omasum, where water and minerals are absorbed from it. The fourth chamber, the abomasum, is most like the one-chambered stomach of nonruminant animals. It produces enzymes that digest the fats and proteins in the stomach contents, including the microorganisms that have absorbed nutrients from the cellulose. A significant part of the deer's nutrition, in fact, comes from the microorganisms. The colonies of microorganisms in the deer's rumen and reticulum, however, continuously renew themselves.

The stomach contents leave the abomasum through an opening called the pyloric valve, which connects to the intestine. As the material travels down the intestine, water is absorbed, along with the remaining nutrients it carries. The rest of the material leaves the body through the anal opening as dung, or solid waste. Because the cervid digestive system extracts much of the liquid—and the nutrients it contains—before the waste leaves the body, deer dung is usually dry and compact. Food passes through a human digestive system in about a day. But depending on the amount of cellulose in a deer's food, it can take several days for a deer's digestive system to process a meal.

Sharp Senses

Deer are well adapted to fleeing from predators, but first they must be aware of them. In addition to their running and jumping abilities, deer have keen senses that alert them to potential dangers. They have excellent hearing, helped by large, movable pinnae, or outer ears. The pinnae capture sounds and direct them into the inner ear. Deer can tilt and rotate their pinnae through a wide range of motion and can even move them in separate directions at the same time. This allows them to listen to sounds coming from all directions. The source of a sound is usually a bit farther from one ear than from the other, so it reaches one ear a fraction of a second before the other. This tiny difference helps the deer pinpoint the location of the sound. If a group of deer are grazing and something nearby rustles some leaves, or snaps a dry twig, the deers' heads will snap up and turn in the same direction, immediately looking toward the source of the disturbance.

Deer have good eyesight, although it is not like human eyesight. For a long time, deer were believed to be color-blind. Recent studies of fallow deer, a kind of deer found in many parts of the world, suggest that deer do have some ability to perceive color, but it may not be very well developed. Deer are also not very good at seeing shapes and patterns beyond a distance of about 165 to 200 feet (50 to 60 meters). What they are good at, however, is seeing motion in their field of vision. Deer can detect even small movements at distances of up to 660 to 990 feet (200 to 300 meters), depending upon the species. Their eyesight is adapted to meet the needs of their herbivorous way of life. It is less important for deer to have a crisp, detailed picture of their environment than it is for them to pick up flickers of motion that might be telltale signs of a predator approaching. In addition, deer see better in low light than humans do. A deer's visual picture of the world is limited but highly specialized.

Smell contributes a great deal to a deer's awareness of the environment around it. A deer's olfaction, or sense of smell, is very acute. Researchers believe that deer use their sense of smell in three ways: to locate desirable foods, to pick up olfactory cues about possible predators, and to communicate with each other. Deer use olfactory information not just to recognize each other but also to advertise themselves to possible mates, to mark their territories, and to issue challenges to each other. A deer that spots a predator may produce a scent-mark that indicates alarm or danger in that place.

Deer receive olfactory information through two sense organs. One is the nasal membrane inside the nose. The other is the vomeronasal organ on the roof of the mouth. Both are

A SCOTTISH RED DEER IS FLEHMENING, DRAWING AIR OVER CELLS IN ITS MOUTH THAT SENSE CHEMICAL TRACES IN THE AIR. CATS, HORSES, AND MANY OTHER ANIMALS USE FLEHMENING, OFTEN WHEN THEY ARE MATING OR MARKING TERRITORY.

sensitive to scent molecules in the air, and both send information about those signals to the brain. To draw air—and scent molecules—over the vomeronasal organ, a deer may do what scientists call flehmen breathing, or flehmening. It involves curling back the upper lip, opening the mouth, and sucking in air.

To produce scents that other deer can "read," deer use two things: their scent glands and their urine. Scent glands produce liquid or waxy substances filled with scent molecules. All deer have preorbital scent glands, which are located just in front of the eyes. Some species also have scent glands on the forehead. Deer spread the scent from these glands by rubbing their faces on trees and other vegetation. Other glands are located between the toes. These are called interdigital glands on the front feet and intertarsal glands on the hind feet. They leave an invisible trail of scent as deer move about, helping the animals keep track of one another.

In some species, such as the musk deer, males have a preputial gland, which is a scent gland near the sheath of skin that covers the penis. During mating season, the preputial gland produces a substance called musk that is highly prized by perfume makers. Many species of deer also have tarsal glands, located on the hind legs of both males and females. Tufts of slightly longer hair mark the location of these glands, which do not produce scent molecules; instead, they make a fatty substance that coats the hairs. Both male and female deer rub their hind legs together as they urinate. This action, called rub-urination, coats the hairs of the tarsal gland with urine, which sticks to the fatty substance. Bacteria act on the combination of urine and fat to produce a strong odor.

Urine has other uses in communication among deer. Many species of deer leave scent markings by scraping the grounds and then urinating on the scrapes. Males of species that have

A MUDDY OR WATERY WALLOW COVERS A DEER'S COAT WITH SCENT. WALLOWING MAY ALSO SOOTHE INSECT BITES AND GIVE SOME PROTECTION AGAINST SKIN PARASITES.

long or shaggy neck hair, such as elk and red deer, may urinate on their own necks to soak the hairs with their scent, which they spread about by rubbing against trees. Elk, moose, red deer, and many other kinds of deer also wallow. The males use their antlers to tear up patches of earth, then urinate on the earth to moisten it, creating a muddy patch called a wallow. Rolling around in the wallow, the deer mixes the scent from his foot and leg glands into the mud. The wallowing also coats the deer with the scented mud, which he then rubs on trees to attract females.

Moose (known as elk in Europe) spend a lot of time in ponds, lakes, and marshes, feeding on water plants. Their antlers are palmated—broad and flat, with tines sticking up like fingers from the palm of a hand.

Unique Antlers

Antlers may be the most distinctive feature of the deer families. Other animals, including cattle, goats, and antelope, have permanent horns, but only cervids grow bone antlers each year, then shed them and regrow them the following year. Even within the deer families, though, a few species—the musk deer and Chinese water deer—do not have antlers.

Deer exhibit a quality that scientists call sexual dimorphism, which means that there are visible differences between males and females, apart from the differences of their reproductive systems. In most deer species, size is one kind of sexual dimorphism. Females are almost always smaller than males, although in some species the difference is hard to see without measuring the animals. Sexual dimorphism also appears in antlers, which grow only on male deer, with a single exception. The caribou, or reindeer, *Rangifer tarandus*, is the only species in which both males and females have antlers.

Antlers grow from a pair of bone bases called pedicles, which are located on the deer's forehead. The antlers are made of bone. As they grow, they are surrounded and nourished by their velvet, a coating of skin that contains blood vessels. Once an antler is fully developed, the blood vessels at the base of the pedicle close up. The velvet dries up, dies, and falls off in tatters. Deer often scrape their antlers against trees to loosen and remove the velvet; this can leave dried blood on the antlers but does not appears to be painful to the deer. The deer wears the antlers for about eight months or so, then—usually in fall or winter—the antlers are cast, or shed. Each antler separates from its pedicle and falls off. A deer does not necessarily lose both antlers at the same time, but they usually fall off within a day or two of each other.

Scientists believe that the annual cycle of growing and casting antlers is governed by the male hormone testosterone, which is present, in varying amounts, in both male and female deer. When testosterone rises to a certain level, the antlers begin to develop. Usually they are fully formed by mating season. Some time afterward, the level of testosterone in the deer's system falls below a certain level, and the antlers are cast. In reindeer, however, the formation of antlers in both sexes appears to be governed by something other than testosterone, perhaps other hormones or a genetic mutation.

Antlers become larger, and often more elaborately branched, with each year that a male deer approaches maturity. Although antlers take a variety of shapes, all of them develop in much the same way. The main branch of the antler, called the beam, grows first. Secondary branches may sprout from it; later, points called tines grow upward or outward from the branches. Moose and fallow deer have palmated antlers, with broad, flat surfaces that resemble the palm of a hand. Tines grow outward from these surfaces.

From the first bump on the pedicle to the tip of the last tines, antlers generally form in twelve to sixteen weeks. Growing antlers takes a lot of energy, and also a lot of calcium and other minerals—deer sometimes gnaw on mineral-rich soil to obtain the materials needed to build a new pair of antlers. So why do cervids grow them? Partly for defense against predators, but mostly, biologists think, for use in activities that are connected with mating.

Deer species that tend to live solitary lives, and species in which males mate with only one or a few females, generally have small, simple antlers. The muntjacs of Asia and pudu of South America, for example, are small forest deer with antlers that are plain spikes. At the other end of the scale, the biggest and most elaborate antlers appear in larger species where animals live in social groups, and males compete to impregnate as many females as possible. Reindeer, or caribou, are typical of this group. Their antlers can be extremely complex, with more than three dozen points. For male deer of these species, antlers are like billboards. They advertise their owners' vigor and general fitness to both females and rival males. Males competing for females display their antlers to each other, each trying to dominate the other, and they sometimes use the antlers to fight each other. Like the peacock's brilliant plumage, the majestic antlers of the deer have evolved to give it an edge in the mating game.

2 Origins, Ancestors, and Relatives

Paleontology, the study of ancient life-forms through fossils, used to be the only source of information about the origins of deer. Today the science of genetics, which uses DNA to examine the relationships among groups of living things, provides new insights into the development of cervids.

Deer are a relatively young group of animals, at least in terms of the long history of life. The ancestors of modern deer were forest-dwelling animals that appeared 15 or 20 million years ago. Over time, as these animals migrated into new parts of the world, they adapted to new habitats and climates. Although the largest cervids that ever lived became extinct along the way, the end result was the diverse deer families of today.

PREHISTORIC CAVE PAINTINGS REVEAL THAT OUR DISTANT ANCESTORS HUNTED DEER WITH BOWS AND ARROWS, AS SOME MODERN SPORT HUNTERS STILL DO. BY THE TIME HUMAN HUNTERS APPEARED, HOWEVER, DEER HAD EXISTED FOR MILLIONS OF YEARS.

Ruminant Evolution

Paleontologists think that cervids are one of many groups of modern mammals that descended from a group of ancient mammals called the condylarths. The condylarths themselves descended from small, insect-eating mammals that existed alongside the dinosaurs. After the dinosaurs became extinct, during the period that scientists call the Paleocene epoch, between 65 million and 55 million years ago, the condylarths developed into many new forms. Some of these forms seem to have been herbivores. One of the earliest, *Protoungulatum*, had teeth that would have allowed it to eat soft plants and fruits as well as insects. Paleontologists consider it a distant ancestor of modern ungulates, or hoofed mammals, including deer.

The Eocene epoch started approximately 50 million years ago. By that time, hoofed mammals evolved into several sub-groups. One of these groups was the artiodactyls, animals with two hoofed toes on each foot. Artiodactyls are sometimes called the cloven-hoofed or split-hoofed mammals, although their two hooves were always separate. One of the earliest known artiodactyls is called *Diacodexis*, found in fossil deposits in Europe, Asia, and North America. It appeared around 54 million years ago. *Diacodexis* was about 20 inches (50 centimeters) long, the size of a large rabbit, with long, slender legs and powerful hip muscles. Its body type suggests that it was cursorial, like some modern ruminants, including deer. The oreodonts, another group of early artiodactyls, evolved during the Eocene epoch. Similar in size and shape to modern sheep, the oreodonts survived into the Oligocene epoch, which began around 34 million years ago, before becoming extinct.

Artiodactyl evolution took off during the late Oligocene epoch, and new groups of artiodactyls continued to develop into the Miocene epoch, which started about 23 million years ago. The ancestors of pigs and camels appeared, and so did the first ruminants, which evolved along with a changing landscape. During the Miocene epoch, the climate over much of the world grew gradually cooler and drier than it had been during the Oligocene and Eocene epochs. One result of this climate change was that, in many regions, forest was replaced by grassland. The spread of grasslands encouraged the evolution of animals that could feed on grasses and on the bushes and shrubs that grow in the border zones where grassland and forest meet. Conditions were ideal for the emergence of ruminants.

The earliest ruminants were small, and their stomachs were not as complex as in most modern ruminants. Miocene fossils show, however, that by 15 million years ago, ruminants had diversified into many distinct lines, the ancestral forms of cattle, goats, antelope, giraffes, and deer. Many small forms of artiodactyls, meanwhile, disappeared.

Based on the fossil record, paleontologists think that deer evolved in Eurasia, the large land mass that contains both Europe and Asia, and later migrated to North America. At first they were creatures of the temperate zone, the area between the tropics and the Arctic. Eventually some deer species colonized the tropics and the Arctic, but the majority of species remained—and still remain today—in the temperate zone of the Northern Hemisphere. By several million years ago, many varieties of modern deer had appeared.

The Extinct Irish Elk

Moose date from about 2.6 million years ago, reindeer from 1 million years ago. These species are still around, but some of the deer that once shared their world have become extinct. The

SCIENTISTS OF EARLIER GENERATIONS HOPED TO FIND IRISH ELK LIVING IN REMOTE PARTS OF THE WORLD. EVENTUALLY THEY REALIZED THAT THE SPECIES HAD VANISHED, AND *MEGALOCEROS* BECAME ONE OF THE FIRST WELL-KNOWN EXAMPLES OF EXTINCTION.

most spectacular of these vanished cervids is *Megaloceros giganteus*, better known as the Irish elk, which mystified generations of scientists.

The Irish elk was the largest deer known to science. It was 7 feet (2.1 meters) tall at the shoulder, with antlers that measured 12 feet (3.6 meters) from side to side and weighed as much as 90 pounds (41 kilograms). In comparison, the largest living species of deer is *Alces alces*, which is known as the moose in

North America and the elk in Europe. Although the biggest bull moose are similar in size to the Irish elk, the moose's antlers are much smaller, with a maximum weight of about 66 pounds (30 kilograms). The width of a moose's antlers seldom measures much more than the moose's height, but the Irish elk sported huge, palmated antlers that were much wider than the animal was tall. According to Rory Putman, the author of *The Natural History of Deer* (1988), the Irish elk's antlers probably weighed more than the rest of the skeleton together.

The Irish elk's name is misleading. Europeans thought it was an elk—the name they use for the animal that Americans call a moose—but it was not. Nor was it the same animal that Americans call an elk or wapiti. *Megaloceros* was not closely related to any living species of cervid, and it was not limited to Ireland. Its range extended across Europe, northern Africa, and northern Asia. But *Megaloceros* was first known from many well-preserved remains found in Ireland, where the enormous antlers were prized as decorations for castles and manor houses. Charles II, king of England in the late seventeenth century, once received a pair of the antlers as a gift. The king had them hung in a gallery at his Hampton Court palace with other hunting trophies. The Irish elk antlers were so much bigger than the rest of the horns and antlers that visitors lost interest in the others.

By that time, the Irish elk was attracting the attention of learned Europeans who puzzled over the fact that, although many of its antlers had been found in lakes and bogs, the Irish elk itself was nowhere to be seen. No one believed that a species could "be lost *entirely* out of the World," as a scholar named Thomas Molyneux wrote in 1697 about the Irish elk. People just assumed that the Irish elk was still alive in other parts of the world. Yet as time went on and Europeans explored more of the world, no one ever came home with a freshly caught Irish elk. Not until 1812 did a French naturalist named Georges Cuvier prove, through a detailed comparison of *Megaloceros* fossils and the skeletons of living cervids, that the Irish elk was unlike any living deer. Together with the growing recognition that the earth was full of creatures that no longer existed, Cuvier's study of the Irish elk helped to establish the reality of extinction.

Once scientists had accepted that *Megaloceros* was extinct, they wondered why it had disappeared. The main theory of the nineteenth century was that the antlers killed the elk. Evolution had made the antlers larger and larger, according to this theory, until they were simply too big for the elk's good. Various experts suggested that the Irish elk died out because all the males got their antlers stuck between trees in the forest, or sank under the weight of their antlers in swamps and lakes, or had their necks broken by the weight of the antlers.

Evolution is better understood today. Scientists know that a species would not continue to evolve antlers that were so large that they killed off their wearers. The real cause of the elk's disappearance was most likely climate change connected with the final phases of the last Ice Age. The elk was one of many species of large mammals that became extinct around 11,000 years ago, either because of a final period of very cold weather or because the grassland habitat was replaced by forest when the glaciers withdrew. As for the elk's giant antlers, scientists think that the males displayed them to potential mates and rivals, just as cervids do today.

When Is a Deer Not a Deer?

Mouse deer, native to Asia and Africa, can be seen in many zoos worldwide. The largest species lives in Africa. It stands about 18

A BOY IN THE PHILIPPINES HOLDS A MOUSE DEER, OR CHEVROTAIN. THESE SMALL
MAMMALS APPEAR IN FOLK TALES IN MANY PARTS OF ASIA, WHERE PEOPLE EAT THEM
AND ALSO KEEP THEM AS PETS.

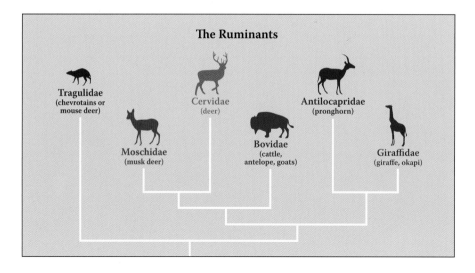

The Ruminants

Tragulidae
(chevrotains or
mouse deer)

Cervidae
(deer)

Antilocapridae
(pronghorn)

Moschidae
(musk deer)

Bovidae
(cattle,
antelope, goats)

Giraffidae
(giraffe, okapi)

SCIENTISTS THINK THAT THE EVOLUTIONARY LINE LEADING TO THE CHEVROTAINS SPLIT
OFF VERY EARLY FROM THE LINE LEADING TO ALL OTHER RUMINANTS. PRONGHORNS AND
THE GIRAFFE FAMILY ARE MORE CLOSELY RELATED THAN EITHER IS TO THE REST OF THE
RUMINANTS: CATTLE, GOATS, ANTELOPE, AND THE TWO FAMILIES OF DEER.

inches (46 centimeters) tall at the shoulder and weighs 22 to
26.5 pounds (10 to 12 kilograms). The Asian species are smaller—full-grown adults may be no bigger than a large cat. Mouse
deer have long legs, reddish-brown fur that is striped and spotted with white, and deerlike heads. They have no antlers,
although the males possess short tusks. These appealing little
animals do look like miniature deer, but they are neither deer
nor mice. They are chevrotains.

The half-dozen or so species of chevrotains are the world's
smallest ungulates. Like deer, chevrotains are artiodactyls and
ruminants, but the chambers of their stomachs are not as fully
developed as in other ruminants. Paleontologists used to think
that deer evolved from chevrotains. Some now believe that,
although the earliest deer may have resembled chevrotains, the

chevrotains split off from the main line of ruminant evolution before deer developed. Taxonomists, scientists who organize and classify the forms of life, have placed chevrotains in their own family, Tragulidae. For this reason these shy, secretive, forest-dwelling creatures are sometimes called tragulids.

Classifying Modern Deer

The scientific classification of deer has changed often in recent years as researchers have reexamined the relationships among deer. Musk deer, for example, were traditionally considered a subfamily within the family Cervidae, but many scientists now place them in a separate family, the Moschidae. There are also several different ways of classifying the Cervidae into subfamilies. No single system of taxonomy is accepted by all researchers.

Even the total number of deer species depends upon which expert is asked. The average taxonomy, however, contains about five species of Moschidae and forty-four species of Cervidae. Both families are contained in the suborder Ruminantia, which in turn is contained in the order Artiodactyla of the class Mammalia, or mammals.

3 Types of Deer Today

In terms of the number of species, deer are the most successful hoofed animals in the Americas. Some fifteen species of cervids are found in North, Central, and South America, more than for any other ungulate. Africa, in contrast, is dominated by the bovid family of cattle, antelope, and their relatives. It has only one cervid, *Cervus elaphus,* or the red deer, and the deer's range is limited to the northwestern corner of the continent. The greatest variety of deer is found in the part of the world where deer originated: Eurasia, which has more than thirty species. One entire family, the Moschidae, lives only in Asia.

Musk Deer

Many scientists recognize five species of Moschidae—the Himalayan, Nepal, Chinese, forest, and Siberian musk deer. All five favor densely wooded habitats in mountainous areas. The Siberian musk deer ranges as far north as the Arctic Circle.

A SIBERIAN MUSK DEER SLIPS THROUGH THE FOREST OF A DEER SANCTUARY IN INDIA. BOTH MALE AND FEMALE MUSK DEER HAVE TWO SMALL DOWNWARD-POINTING TUSKS.

Several other species can be found in southern China and the Himalayas, while the forest musk deer is found in the subtropical jungles of northern Vietnam and Myanmar.

In most deer species, males are noticeably larger than females. Musk deer females, however, are about the same size as males, sometimes larger. Depending on the species, musk deer weigh between 22 and 33 pounds (10 and 15 kilograms) and stand 19.5 to 31 inches (49.5 to 78.4 centimeters) tall at the shoulder. With powerful hip muscles and hind legs slightly longer than their front legs, musk deer are powerful jumpers and fast saltatorial runners. They are also excellent climbers. Unlike other kinds of deer, musk deer have long dewclaws that touch the ground. These assist the deer in climbing and clinging to steep surfaces.

Creatures of habit, musk deer create networks of trails that they regularly follow through their territory, which usually measures 1 to 1.5 miles (1.6 to 2.4 kilometers) from side to side. Each territory is home to a pair of deer. Musk deer are crepuscular, which means that they are most active at dawn and dusk. During the middle of the day and at night they rest in a nestlike hollow in the forest floor, usually sleeping in the same place every day.

Musk deer have often been called the most "primitive" living deer. Scientists today are more likely to say that musk deer retain more of the ancestral features than other modern deer do. In some ways musk deer resemble chevrotains. Like chevrotains, they lack antlers. Male and female musk deer, however, have two upper teeth that have developed into curving, downward-pointing tusks that may reach 4 inches (10 centimeters) in length. Another feature shared with chevrotains is a somewhat simplified stomach structure. The rumen of a musk deer's stomach is less well developed than those of species in the family Cervidae.

The musk deer's unique physical feature has almost brought about its destruction. A gland possessed by males of all species yields a brown, waxy substance called musk. Since ancient times, musk has been used as a base for perfumes, soaps, and folk medicines. It is one of the costliest substances on earth. Although it is possible to harvest musk from the deer without killing them, most deer that are hunted for the musk trade die in traps and snares. Wildlife experts estimate that, during the 1990s, as many as half a million Moschidae were killed for their musk each year. People in China and India are raising musk deer in captivity in order to supply the market with musk while allowing wild populations of the deer to recover, but it is too soon to say how successful these operations will be. International demand for musk is expected to remain strong. Even if the trade in wild musk is officially banned, people in remote areas will probably continue hunting the deer as long as they can find buyers for the musk.

Chinese Water Deer

The family Cervidae is divided into four subfamilies. One of them, Hydropotinae, has only one species, the Chinese water deer. Like the musk deer, the Chinese water deer lacks antlers but has short tusks. It also resembles musk deer in its size, body structure, and bounding gait.

Native to Korea and northeastern China, the Chinese water deer favors open habitat such as moist grasslands, marshes, and the beds of reeds and bushes along lakeshores and riverbanks. It is a strong swimmer and feeds on many kinds of water plants, but it also likes food crops such as grain and vegetables, and this brings it into frequent conflict with farmers.

Throughout the range of the Chinese water deer, people have exterminated nearly all of its natural predators, tigers and

MOIST GRASSLANDS NEAR WATER ARE THE FAVORITE HABITAT OF THE CHINESE WATER DEER.

wolves. Its major predators are now domestic and feral dogs. The same is true in France and England. Both nations have populations of water deer, descended from animals that have escaped from private game parks and zoos.

Muntjacs

Muntjacs are small forest deer of southern and eastern Asia. They are one reason for the variety in deer taxonomies. Some scientists group muntjacs with the larger subfamily of Eurasian

Sometimes called the Chinese muntjac, Reeve's muntjac is one of the larger varieties of muntjac. The species is named for John Reeves, an Englishman who introduced these deer to Britain in the nineteenth century. Today they are found in dense, brushy woodland thickets in Britain as well as in many parts of East Asia.

deer. The majority of experts, though, consider muntjacs to be a separate subfamily called the Cervulinae or Muntiacinae.

Scientists do not agree on how many species of muntjacs there are. Figures range from six to twelve, depending upon whether the biologist in question is a lumper (tending to lump similar animals into a single species unless the reasons for splitting them into multiple species are strong) or a splitter (tending to see slight differences as grounds for naming separate species).

In the 1990s, two new species of muntjac were discovered in the hill country of Southeast Asia—the giant muntjac in northern Vietnam and the leaf deer or leaf muntjac in Myanmar. The giant muntjac, *Muntiacus vuquangensis*, is the largest member of the subfamily. Males weigh up to 72.6 pounds (33 kilograms) and may be 30.5 inches (78 centimeters) tall at the shoulder.

One member of the muntjac subfamily, the tufted deer, lives in mountainous regions of southern Tibet, northern Myanmar, and southern China at altitudes of up to 14,760 feet (4,500 meters) above sea level. The other muntjac species live at lower altitudes in China and Southeast Asia. They are usually found below 5,000 feet (1,525 meters).

Sometimes called barking deer because of the loud, sharp warning cries they make when they are alarmed, muntjacs are crepuscular, territorial, trail-making animals, like musk deer. Unlike musk deer, though, they have antlers. The tufted deer's antlers are short and often hidden by the tufts of long hair that give the deer its name. The other species have antlers that grow out of distinctively long pedicles. The average male muntjac's pedicles are about 6 inches (15 centimeters) long, so that even after the deer has shed its antlers it still appears to have skin-covered horns. Male muntjacs also have short tusks. Like musk deer and Chinese water deer, male muntjacs sometimes fight with their tusks, trying to slash each other's sides.

Eurasian Deer

The subfamily Cervinae contains the deer species that are native to Europe and Asia, as well as one species that also occurs in North America and Africa. Some of the species in Cervinae have many subspecies, varieties that live in different geographic areas and have slight physical differences. Subspecies can interbreed with each other because they are all members of the same species, yet they seldom do so in the wild because they are geographically separate.

THIS RED DEER HIND, OR FEMALE, AND HER FAWN BELONG TO A SPECIES THAT HAS BEEN HIGHLY PRIZED AS A GAME ANIMAL FOR CENTURIES. BECAUSE OF ITS IMPORTANCE TO HUNTERS, THE RED DEER IS ONE OF THE MOST STUDIED AND MANAGED SPECIES OF WILDLIFE IN THE WORLD.

The red deer, *Cervus elaphus*, may have the most extensive range of any deer species. Its natural range extends from northwestern Africa, where it is known as the Barbary deer, to eastern Tibet, where it is called the shou. Red deer are found in the British Isles, Scandinavia, the Mediterranean islands of Corsica and Sardinia, Central and Eastern Europe, Turkey, Iran, Afghanistan, Kashmir in the Himalayas, and Central Asia.

Reddish-brown in summer, red deer turn darker brown or grayish in winter. Stags, as male red deer are called, have long, shaggy dark hair on their necks. The largest stags are found in Eastern Europe and can reach shoulder heights of 58 inches (150 centimeters) and weights of up to 750 pounds (340 kilograms). Hinds, or female red deer, are usually about three-fourths the size of stags.

Red deer occupy a variety of habitats, from forests to river basins to grasslands. They are social cervids, forming herds that feed together, usually in the early morning, the late morning, and the evening. For most of the year, hinds and stags are in separate herds. They spend time together only during mating season.

For centuries the red deer has been the most desired game animals, and the most heavily hunted, in most of its range. Red deer have a long association with nobility and the upper-class sport of hunting. In Europe they were considered the rightful quarry of noble hunters; commoners were forbidden to hunt red deer and had to content themselves with less prestigious species of deer. Today many red deer in Eurasia live on privately owned forests, estates, or hunting parks. Others live in protected forests or wildlife preserves. They have been imported as game animals to Australia, New Zealand, North America, Argentina, and Chile.

Red deer belong to the genus *Cervus*. The genus contains ten other species, all similar in appearance and habits to the red deer. *Cervus canadensis*, for example, is much like a red deer,

except that it is larger and has a golden-brown coat. It is found
in China, Mongolia, Siberia, North Korea, and the Central Asian
republics of Kazakhstan and Kyrgyzstan. It also lives in many
parts of western Canada and the United States, where it is called
the American elk or wapiti. *Cervus nippon*, the Japanese deer,
or sika, is like a slightly smaller version of the red deer, with a
stocky body and a dark brown coat. The sika's natural range
includes parts of China, Siberia, Korea, and Southeast Asia in
addition to China. Sika have been transplanted to Europe and
the United States as well, and wild herds now exist in both
regions. In the United States, they have become established in
areas of the East Coast, such as Maryland and Virginia.

THOROLD'S DEER STANDS ABOUT 4 FEET (1.25 METERS) TALL AT THE SHOULDER AND WEIGHS 285 TO 310 POUNDS (130 TO 140 KILOGRAMS). IT IS SOMETIMES CALLED THE WHITE-LIPPED DEER BECAUSE PART OF THE MUZZLE IS WHITE IN MANY INDIVIDUALS.

Other *Cervus* species include the Thorold's deer of Tibet, the sambar of India and eastern Asia, the barasingha or swamp deer of India and Nepal, and the Eld's deer, or thamin, of Myanmar and Thailand. The Eld's deer favors swampy, marshy habitats and has a distinctive adaptation to help it walk on soft, soggy ground. It is the only deer species whose weight is supported by its pasterns (the bottom of the ankle, just above the hoof) in addition to its hooves.

The *Axis* genus of Eurasian deer contains four species. The best known is the axis, or chital deer, which inhabits lowlands in India and Nepal; its natural habitat is the woodland border or

Bawean and Calamian deer, are more solitary. All four species rest during the middle of the day to avoid being overstressed by heat. If temperatures remain high for any length of time, the deer adapt by becoming active at night. All of the *Axis* species have deep reddish-brown coats with vivid white spots. Many deer are born with spots, but axis deer, unlike most, keep the spots throughout their lives.

The third genus in the Cervinae subfamily, *Dama*, contains the fallow deer. Some taxonomists consider all fallow deer to be one species, while others recognize a second species, the Persian fallow deer. Originally native to the eastern Mediterranean region, Iran, Turkey, and southern Europe, fallow deer have had their range enlarged by humans over hundreds of years. Imported to parks and preserves in Asia, England, Australia, New Zealand, and the Americas, fallow deer have established wild populations in many of those places.

Fallow deer have more varieties of coloring than any other deer. The most common coloring is white-spotted reddish brown in summer and grayish-brown with faint spots in winter, but fallow deer also occur in black, blue-gray, and white versions. Some white fallow deer are albinos, with red eyes, but others have normal, dark brown eyes. Where fallow deer live in forested habitat, they tend to be solitary or to form small groups. In their preferred habitat of grassland bordered by forest, however, they sometimes feed and travel together in herds of as many as thirty animals.

The fourth and last genus of Cervinae, *Elaphurus*, contains just one species, Père David's deer. Some experts consider this large deer to be a close relative of the *Cervus* genus, but Père David's deer has several unusual features. The tines of its antlers point back and down instead of forward and up as on all other deer. Père David's deer also has broad, widely splayed hooves. Caribou and reindeer, which have similar hooves, are adapted

THE CHINESE EMPERORS' PRIVATE PARKS ALLOWED PÈRE DAVID'S DEER TO ESCAPE EXTINCTION. NOW THIS DEER IS BEING RETURNED TO THE WILD IN CHINA.

to walk on snow—their broad hooves spread the weight of the animal over a large area and keep its feet from sinking into the snow. Perhaps Père David's deer also evolved to travel over snow, or maybe it is adapted to muddy or boggy terrain. The question cannot be answered for sure, because almost nothing is known about the animal's natural habitat.

The story of Père David's deer is a good example of how humans and deer have interacted over the centuries. In 1865 a French missionary named Armand David got a glimpse into the imperial hunting park of the Chinese royal family, south of Beijing. Heavily guarded, surrounded by a 45-mile (72-kilometer) wall, the park was off limits to all but the emperor and his companions and attendants. But David was curious, so he bribed a guard to let him take a quick peep over the wall. He saw a large herd of strange-looking deer. Thinking that they might be an unknown type of reindeer, David managed—with the help of more bribes—-to get hold of two of their skins. He sent them to Paris, where a zoologist examined them and pronounced them a new species, which he named after the determined David.

Within a few years, China shared information about Père David's deer with the rest of the world. According to brief references in ancient Chinese histories, the species was once native to northern China and Korea. It became extinct in wild long ago, perhaps as early as the third century B.C.E. ore that happened, however, China's imperial family had cted several herds for the hunting park. There the spe rvived for more than two thousand years.

China presented some of the deer to zo nd private collectors in Europe. This was fortunate, bec e at the end of the nineteenth century the imperial huntir rk was destroyed by massive floods that killed all of its P David's deer. The owners of the European herds start reeding program to preserve and strengthen captive ulations in England, France, and Germany. The progra peen successful, and in the late twentieth century, seve ds of Père David's deer were sent to China. Wildlife rities there are experimenting with returning the spe the wild in parts of its former range.

American Deer

The f n species of deer found in the Americas are grouped together in the subfamily Odocoileinae (some taxonomists give this subfamily the name Capreolinae). Although they are generally called "American deer," the term is not completely accurate.

THIS YOUNG ROE DEER BUCK'S ANTLERS WILL BECOME LARGER EACH YEAR.

Two of the species are found in Eurasia as well as the Americas. The subfamily also includes one species, the roe deer, that is found only in Eurasia and not in the Americas. Even though the roe deer does not share a range with the American deer, it is genetically related to them. Some scientists think that the roe deer may be the living species that is most closely related to the ancestral line of all American deer.

The roe deer is found across Eurasia, from England and Scotland in the West to China and Korea in the East. Roe deer are widely hunted, but because they are of great interest to sport hunters they are also monitored, managed, and conserved, at least in Europe.

Roe deer are on the small side, ranging from 25 to 35.5 inches (65 to 90 centimeters) high at the shoulder and weighing between 33 and 75 pounds (15 to 34 kilograms). The larger individuals are usually found east of Russia's Ural Mountains. Some experts consider the animals in this eastern part of the range to be a separate subspecies or even a separate species.

When roe deer are able to live in their preferred habitat of dense woodland, they are solitary. The loss of forest habitat in much of their range has led roe deer to move into more open types of ecosystems, such as meadows and parklands, where they sometimes feed in loosely joined herds. Roe deer are good swimmers and jumpers, but they cannot run fast or for long periods, so they favor environments with a lot of cover—dense undergrowth, tall grass, or brushy thickets—where they can hide when danger threatens.

Two species of deer in the Odocoileinae subfamily are in the northern parts of both North America and Eurasia. They are *Alces alces*, called moose in America and elk in Europe, and *Rangifer tarandus*, known as caribou in America and reindeer in Europe. Most experts divide each species into three or more subspecies.

Moose, the largest deer, are found throughout Alaska and Canada. In the lower forty-eight states they occur in New England, New York, the upper Midwest, and the Rocky Mountains. Their Eurasian range extends from Scandinavia and the Baltic region across northern Russia and Siberia. The

ALCES ALCES, THE WORLD'S LARGEST DEER, IS A MOOSE IN NORTH AMERICA AND AN ELK IN EUROPE. IN THE SCANDINAVIAN NATION OF SWEDEN, ARCHAEOLOGISTS HAVE FOUND EVIDENCE THAT STONE AGE HUNTERS USED PITS TO TRAP AND KILL *A. ALCES* AS EARLY AS EIGHT THOUSAND YEARS AGO.

traditional lifestyles of many Native American and Siberian peoples include subsistence hunting for moose; these large animals are also prized by sport hunters.

Their distinctive appearance sets moose apart from most other deer species. In addition to being large, moose are very long-legged, an adaptation that probably helps them move through the winter snows in their northerly range and also equips them to wade in lakes and ponds, where they feed on water plants. Moose have large muzzles with big, overhanging upper lips. The skin of their lips is thick and tough, inside and out, which lets moose use the feeding technique of pulling a branch of a bush, shrub, or young tree through their lips, stripping off all the leaves. Beneath a moose's throat dangles a flap of skin called a dewlap. A narrow strip of skin as long as 18 inches (45.7 centimeters), called the rope, often hangs down from the dewlap. Scientists do not know the purpose of either the dewlap or the rope. They do know, however, that not all moose

WHETHER IT IS CALLED CARIBOU OR REINDEER, *RANGIFER TARANDUS* IS VITAL TO THE TRADITIONAL LIFESTYLES OF HUNTING AND HERDING PEOPLES IN THE ARCTIC REGIONS OF NORTH AMERICA AND EURASIA.

have ropes. Some moose lose their ropes when the dangling strips of skin freeze, but that doesn't seem to harm the moose. Generally solitary, moose tend to move around a lot, searching out available food sources. They can move with surprising speed and silence for such large animals. Moose are also excellent swimmers; they paddle with their broad, splayed hooves.

Caribou are descended from reindeer that crossed into North America during periods when glaciers covered much of the earth. Sea levels were lower then, because so much of the planet's water was locked up in the great ice sheets, and Siberia and Alaska were connected by a bridge of land that is now covered by the waters of the Bering Strait. Today caribou and reindeer share some of the moose's range worldwide, but they also live farther north—on some of the northernmost islands of the Canadian Arctic, in the northwest corner of Greenland, and in the far northern reaches of Scandinavia and Siberia. Fossils show that during past Ice Ages, when global temperatures were lower than they are today, caribou lived as far south as Alabama and France.

Caribou and reindeer occupy a variety of habitats, from forest to tundra to open mountain slopes. They show considerable variety in size, with shoulder height ranging from 34 to 54.5 inches (87 to 140 centimeters) and weight ranging from 132 to 700 pounds (60 to 315 kilograms). Reindeer are, in general, smaller than caribou, and females are smaller than males. *Rangifer tarandus* is the only deer species in which females grow antlers, although their antlers are smaller and thinner than those of males. The species is well adapted to life in the cold, with the warmest coat of any cervid. In winter the coat consists of two layers. On the outside are long, air-filled guard hairs that hold air next to the animal's body, where it is warmed by body heat and provides insulation. Beneath the guard hairs is a dense undercoat of fine, woolly fur.

REINDEER ARE THE ONLY CERVIDS THAT HAVE EVER BEEN DOMESTICATED ON A LARGE SCALE. VARIOUS EURASIAN PEOPLES KEEP REINDEER HERDS THAT PROVIDE TRANSPORTATION, MEAT, AND MILK.

Reindeer and caribou make seasonal migrations from winter to summer feeding grounds and back again. Highly social animals, they usually spend the winter in small groups but form large herds, perhaps numbering in the thousands, for the spring migrations. Herds cover between 11 and 34 miles (19 and 55 kilometers) each day. For some herds, the round-trip migration each year involves distances of up to 1,600 miles (2,574 kilometers).

Many species of deer are protected in parks, and people raise some species of deer in captivity for their meat or musk. In addition, a few individual deer have become tame pets. Reindeer, however, are the only deer that have been domesticated on a large scale. Some Eurasian peoples have practiced

THE WHITE-TAILED DEER GETS ITS NAME FROM THE UNDERSIDE OF ITS TAIL, WHICH IT OFTEN HOLDS UP AS IT RUNS.

reindeer herding for centuries. It is still common in the area known as Lapland, which includes the northern parts of Norway, Sweden, and Finland. Reindeer not only provide their herders with milk and meat but also serve as draft animals, pulling sleighs in the winter.

The most common deer in North America are the mule deer and the white-tailed deer. Mule deer are found in nearly all parts of western Canada, the western United States south of Alaska, and northwestern Mexico. They got their name from their large ears, which some people think look like the long ears of mules (the hybrid offspring of donkeys and horses). Mulies, as they are often called, are sturdy, medium-sized deer with reddish-brown summer coats and grayish-brown winter coats. Several subspecies are called black-tailed deer because their tails are black on the upper surface and white below. Mule deer typically spend the summer months feeding in mountain meadows, then migrate to lower, warmer elevations for the winter.

ADAPTED TO LIFE ON SMALL ISLANDS WITH LIMITED HABITAT AND FOOD, THE FLORIDA KEY DEER IS THE SMALLEST WHITETAIL SUBSPECIES.

SMALL AND SHY, BROCKET DEER TEND TO AVOID DANGER BY HIDING IN DENSE THICKETS OR UNDERBRUSH WHEN THEY FEEL THREATENED. COMMON PREDATORS ARE COYOTES, JAGUARS, AND MOUNTAIN LIONS.

The range of the white-tailed deer is larger and more environmentally diverse than that of the mule deer. Whitetails live from southern Canada to northern South America. In the United States, they are found in almost every state but have traditionally been most numerous in the eastern and central parts of the country.

The white-tailed deer is an extremely varied species. Some authorities divide it into as many as thirty-eight subspecies, inhabiting environments that are as geographically and ecologically different as the cold, high valleys of the Canadian Rockies and the tropical jungles of Colombia and Venezuela. Whitetails show a wide range in size, with shoulder heights from 21.4 to 42.9 inches (55 to 100 centimeters) and weights from 40 to 473 pounds (18 to 275 kilograms). In general, the southern sub-species are smaller than the northern ones. In the United States, the smallest subspecies is the Florida Key deer, which inhabits a string of small islands south of Florida.

Aside from the Bawean deer in Indonesia, the only deer whose natural ranges are in the Southern Hemisphere are those that live in South America south of the equator. Some of these southern species are found in the largest genus of American deer, *Mazama*. This group contains four types of brocket deer (some authorities recognize as many as seven or eight species).

The brockets are found in forested habitats from central Mexico to southern Argentina. They are solitary, short-legged deer with simple spikes for antlers. Although they are good

A MARSH DEER PICKS HER WAY THROUGH THE PANTANAL, A REGION OF SWAMPS AND WETLANDS IN SOUTHWESTERN BRAZIL.

THE PUDU, THE WORLD'S SMALLEST DEER, IS NATIVE TO FORESTED PARTS OF CHILE AND ARGENTINA, BUT IT IS NOW BEING RAISED IN SOME OF THE WORLD'S ZOOS.

swimmers and are capable of saltatorial running, brocket deer typically try to avoid trouble by hiding in dense brush or undergrowth. Their diet is highly varied, including water plants, leaves, grasses, fruits, berries, shoots, and many types of mushrooms.

Two other South American species, the marsh deer and the pampas deer, occupy the same range but tend to live in different types of habitat. Both species are found in southern Brazil, Paraguay, Uruguay, and northern Argentina; the pampas deer also lives in Bolivia. Pampas deer are small. Their primary habitat is the pampas, rolling country covered with tall grass and cut by many streambeds. Marsh deer are larger, about the size of whitetails. Their habitat is marshes and swamps, and they spend a lot of time wading and feeding in the water, although they may be driven into hilly districts when their territories are flooded. Marsh deer have distinctive coloration: reddish-gold or reddish-brown coats, with black legs.

Two species of deer live high in the Andes Mountains of western South America. They are the North Andean deer and the South Andean deer, also called the Peruvian huemul and the Chilean huemul (or guemul). Biologists know that when similar species live at different distances from the equator, the one that is farther from the equator, and therefore lives in a cooler climate, is usually larger. This is the true for huemuls—the southern or Chilean species is larger. A male Chilean huemul may measure 35 inches (90 centimeters) at the shoulder and weigh 143 pounds (65 kilograms).

During summer, huemuls graze on grasses and herbs in alpine meadows at altitudes above 13,000 feet (3,960 meters). They move to lower slopes in the winter months. Unlike other deer, male and female huemuls remain paired all the time, not just at mating season. Pairs do not join to form large herds, but they may travel in small family groups that include three generations.

The last of the deer species are the pudu, small, quiet forest deer that are similar in their habits to the musk deer and muntjacs of Asia. Their habitat is dense vegetation. Although they may venture into grasslands or farmers' fields to graze, they seldom go far from their forest territories, where they maintain a network of narrow trails roofed over by brush.

Pudu are the smallest deer in the world, measuring 10 to 16.7 inches (25 and 43 centimeters) tall at the shoulder and weighing 12.7 to 29.4 pounds (6 to 13 kilograms). Despite their small size and their cuteness, pudu are tough little animals. They take to the water or bound over steep rocks to escape predatory dogs, and in mating season the males fight fiercely with antlers, teeth, and hooves. For pudu as for all other deer species, the rhythm of life is defined by the need to find food, avoid predators, and take part in the annual cycle of mating and breeding.

4 Deer Life

In many parts of the world, multiple species of deer share the same range. Red, fallow, roe, and sometimes sika deer live in the same stretches of European countryside. There are places in South America where all four species of brocket deer overlap. The Terai, the lowland jungle region of southern Nepal, is home to chital, sambar, hog deer, and muntjacs. By studying how deer of different species share an environment, scientists have learned a lot about these animals' lives. Despite the fact that all deer share certain basic characteristics, such as being herbivores, a wide range of adaptations has fine-tuned them for different ways of feeding, selecting habitat, raising young, and interacting with each other.

A PAMPAS DEER BUCK, HIS ANTLERS STILL COVERED WITH VELVET, BROWSES ON NEW GROWTH IN A RECENTLY BURNED REGION OF THE CERRADO, A VAST GRASSLAND IN CENTRAL BRAZIL. ALTHOUGH BROWSING CERVIDS CAN SURVIVE ON TOUGH VEGETATION SUCH AS TWIGS AND SHOOTS, SOME SPECIES ARE ATTRACTED TO THE TENDER NEW GROWTH THAT FOLLOWS PERIODIC FIRES.

Food and Habitat

Biologists used to describe deer as either grazers or browsers. Grazers feed mostly on grasses and other ground plants. They typically have broad muzzles, in order to maximize the amount of vegetation they can crop from the ground with each bite, and are associated with grassland habitats. Browsers are woodland species that feed mostly on twig tips, leaves, and vegetation growing off the ground. Their muzzles are narrower, to allow them to nip at selected bites and probe into bushes.

The distinction between grazers and browsers is still useful, but researchers have learned that it is not clear-cut. Many species graze *and* browse, depending on the season and on what food is available to them. Deer can also be described in terms of specialization and opportunism.

Specialists are deer that live in clearly defined habitats and use specific food resources. They are highly adapted to particular circumstances, which gives them the advantage of not having to compete with many rival species for their particular role in the environment. The disadvantage of being a specialist, though, is that a species that depends on a very specific food source or habitat does not always adjust well when circumstances change.

Opportunists, unlike specialists, can survive on a wide range of foods and in a variety of habitats. Although this means that opportunists must compete for resources with a larger number of species, they are more flexible than specialists when circumstances change. For example, opportunists are more likely than specialists to survive habitat loss by colonizing new habitats.

The huemuls of South America's Andes Mountains are specialists. They are adapted to life on mountain slopes and favor open country or shrubland. They feed mostly on grasses and herbs. Only when severe winter conditions drive them downslope into forests do they browse on twig tips. There is no evidence that they have ever enlarged their range or expanded into new habitats. In fact, habitat loss due to human activities such as ranching and mining has endangered both species of huemuls.

The white-tailed deer of the Americas, in contrast, are opportunists. Whitetails are primarily a woodland species, but they have adapted to life in areas of scattered or sparse forest, such as the Great Plains states. In Central and South America, they have become seasonal migrants, spending the dry season in the lowlands near rivers, then withdrawing to higher ground during the rainy season. Whitetails also migrate seasonally in the northern part of their North American range. In fall, as the days grow shorter and winter approaches, whitetails may migrate up to 50 miles (80 kilometers) to a wintering area that is lower or more sheltered, and therefore warmer.

Whitetails have also been highly successful at adapting to the human presence in the landscape. The spread of agriculture has created a new habitat for whitetails in the woodland belts or groves that border croplands in agricultural districts, where the fields provide large quantities of high-quality food. White-tailed deer have also colonized urban parks and suburban neighborhoods, where they are sometimes regarded as pests for eating garden plants and ornamental shrubs and trees. Today, deer populations tend to be denser in agricultural areas and suburbs—both of which are manmade landscapes—than in areas that are mostly forested.

Specialization and opportunism blend in various degrees from one deer species to the next. Europe's roe deer, for example, are specialists in diet and opportunists in habitat. Unlike the red deer that often share their range, roe deer are small and do not require large amounts of food. They are, however, selective feeders. Red deer eat grass, moss, and twigs along with other kinds of vegetation, but roe deer forage for herbs and tender young plant shoots. Pound for pound, they eat less than the red deer, but their food is of higher nutritional value. This means that, although the roe deer requires high-quality forage, the deer can satisfy its food needs within a fairly small territory. Its small size means that it does not need extensive cover. As a result, roe deer have been able to move from their natural forest habitat into agricultural districts, where they can live in hedgerows, thickets, and even ditches. This has enabled roe deer to survive, and sometimes even to thrive, in places where their natural habitat is being lost.

Nepal's Chitwan National Park has been the site of several large studies of how deer species share an environment. Located in the lowlands south of the Himalayas, the park has three kinds of habitat for deer: grassland, riverine forest (brushy forest along river banks), and sal forest (moist tropical forest dominated by the sal tree). Four species of deer inhabit the park: chital, hog deer, sambar, and Indian muntjac. Of these four species, the hog deer makes different use of habitat and resources than the other three. Hog deer in Chitwan National Park are almost entirely creatures of the grassland. The other three species spend the majority of their time in riverine forest, but they use it differently. The solitary muntjac are smaller than the other species, and tend to be selective feeders, like the roe deer. They eat less food than chital and sambar, and they require less cover. Chital tend to gather in herds and feed near the edges of forest areas, where they both browse and graze. Sambar, which spend most of their time alone or in small, loosely linked groups, are opportunistic feeders that are generally found near rivers. They often enter the water to eat water plants. Rarely do any two species compete directly for the same food or cover.

The great variation in the way deer use the resources of their environments allows species to coexist across large parts of the world. It also makes some species more versatile, and therefore more likely to adapt to changing conditions, than others.

Finding a Mate

Courtship and mating follow a variety of patterns among deer species. The small forest deer typically maintain individual territories, and males mate with the females whose territories overlap their own. Studies of animals tagged with radio-transmitting collars have revealed that animals of some solitary species spend more time together than biologists once believed. Both roe deer and muntjacs, for example, are solitary species, yet researchers now know that males and females with overlapping territories frequently associate with each other outside mating season, feeding in the same area.

Wapiti, or American elk, have a mating system in which a male gathers and protects a harem, or group of females. As with all deer species, the wapiti's breeding season begins when females enter a phase called estrus, during which they are fertile. Hormone secretions from their glands and in their urine signal males that the females are ready to breed.

Deer that live in temperate and cold climates, like the wapiti, enter breeding season at the same time each year, in the fall. This means that the young will be born in the spring, giving them a chance to grow during the seasons of good weather and ample food supply. Among these species, many females are

A BULL ELK KEEPS A WATCHFUL EYE ON HIS HAREM OF COWS IN YELLOWSTONE NATIONAL PARK, WYOMING.

likely to enter estrus around the same time. Deer that live the tropics, where temperatures do not change much over the course of a year, may not have a standard breeding season.

Female wapiti spend most of the year living in matriarchal herds led by dominant cows. These female leaders decide where the herds will feed and bed down. Males have their own herds, which also have hierarchies, or pecking orders. The strongest, most dominating bulls are at the top, and the youngest, weakest, or least aggressive are at the bottom. Female and male herds generally avoid each other, except during the three or four weeks of rut, as the breeding season is called. Then males take over the leadership of the female herds, and a frantic time follows.

Bulls do everything they can to attract females, including wallowing, marking territories with scent and urine (this often involves tearing the bark off trees and rubbing against them), and rubbing against pine trees to get odorous resin into their coats. Their goal is to emit the strongest possible smell—and, as many outdoorspeople know, a bull elk in rut can smell very strong indeed.

A bull elk has two main concerns during the breeding season. The first is rounding up as many cows as he can for his personal harem, and he is not always gentle in his methods. Bulls herd cows into their territories by nudging them along, but a cow that does not cooperate risks being gored or raked with the bull's antlers. A successful dominant bull may have a harem of

WHAT STARTS AS A SIMPLE SHOVING MATCH MAY TURN DEADLY IF THE HORNS OF THESE BULL ELK BECOME LOCKED TOGETHER.

twenty-five or more cows. Keeping the harem, however, is the bull's second challenge. He not only has to watch for and chase down runaway cows but also defend his harem from challenges by other bulls. He does this by bugling and by displays of aggression, in which the two bulls walk or run past each other, a few yards or meters apart, demonstrating their antlers. One or both bulls may also stamp the ground and tear at it with the antlers. Usually, one of the bulls backs down.

Conflicts between bull elk rarely reach the point of serious fighting. When fighting does occur, it is likely to be between two younger bulls or between a young bull trying to gain status and an older one trying to hang on to his dominant position. Fights more often involve head-to-head shoving than goring. When death does occur from fighting, it is usually because the two bulls have locked their antlers together and cannot manage to separate them. Joined in a futile struggle, they eventually die of dehydration, starvation, exposure, or predation. This has been known to happen in a number of species that produce complex horns, such as caribou, red deer, and whitetails.

When he is not busy fending off challenges, the bull must tend to his harem, checking each cow to see if she is ready to mate. She signals her readiness by standing still. The bull performs a brief courtship by licking her head and body, after which he mounts her for mating. He will mate with her several times and then turn his attentions to the next cow.

White-tailed deer, mule deer, and moose follow breeding behavior that is different from that of wapiti. For whitetails, rut lasts about two months. Adult bucks follow females who are close to entering estrus. Their persistent pursuit may go one for several days until the doe is ready to mate. If a doe enters estrus, but no bucks are following her, she may seek out a scrape in the ground that a buck has created and urinate into it to signal that she is ready.

Once a buck and doe have paired, he guards her from other bucks by patrolling in a circle around her, chasing off any rivals who try to approach her. Younger bucks without mates can become troublesome at this time. They pursue females—even those that are not in estrus—-and sometimes chase them to the point of exhaustion. Such females may enter the territory of the dominant buck, even though they will not mate, just to have the benefit of his protection.

Family Life

Gestation, the period during which a pregnant female deer carries her unborn young, ranges from 180 days for the Chinese water deer, a small species, to 240 days for the much larger red deer. Shortly before a deer is ready to give birth, she leaves the herd (if she belongs to a social species) and retreats to a birthing area, a secluded spot where she hopes her young will be concealed from predators by vegetation. She drives off other deer that try to enter the birthing area, even her own offspring from earlier births. Female offspring may later rejoin their mother and the newborn young, but males of many species separate from their mothers at this time—and if they don't separate voluntarily, the females drive them away. The young males head off to create their own territories or to join other young males in bachelor herds.

Musk deer, Chinese water deer, and muntjacs often give birth to twins or even triplets. Other Eurasian deer, however, typically bear a single young. Twin births are not uncommon among wapiti, moose, mule deer, and white-tailed deer. Twins

A DOE CLEANS HER NEWBORN FAWN. AS SOON AS THE FAWN CAN WALK, SHE WILL LEAD IT TO ANOTHER SHELTERED SPOT, WHERE IT WILL SPEND ITS FIRST FEW WEEKS.

are likely to occur when females are well-fed and free of stress caused by illness or difficult weather.

Newborn and young deer are called fawns or, in a few species, calves. In nearly all species, they are helpless after birth, unable to walk. The exception is the caribou, or reindeer, the most migratory of all cervids. In this species, all of the pregnant females in a herd give birth to their young within a couple of days of each other. Predators such as grizzly bears, attracted to the newborns as potential food, cannot kill all of them at the same time. This ensures that, although some will be lost, many will survive.

Young caribou can walk almost immediately. By the end of their first week, they can run fast enough to keep up with their mothers. The young of other species are usually able to stand and take a few steps during their first day. As soon as they get to their feet, their mother leads them away from the birthing area, which may draw predators because of blood. She settles them in another resting area, a sheltered spot called a form. If there are two fawns, the doe may place them in separate forms so that, if one is discovered by a predator, the second may remain safe.

Most newborn deer spend their first few weeks of life in the form. Their spotted coats are a kind of protective coloration, giving them the appearance of shadow dappled with patches of sunlight. Does don't tend their fawns nonstop; they leave the form to feed but return often to nurse the young. Fawns instinctively remain still and quiet while the does are away.

After a few days for small species and a few weeks for larger ones, fawns are able to walk and start following their mother around. At this point they either explore their mother's territory, if they belong to solitary species, or join the herd, if they are social. Fawns tend to stick very close to does, tracking their mothers by scent. If necessary, they can follow her at a bounding run.

The next milestone in a young cervid's life is weaning, the end of nursing from the mother. Does and cows begin showing their young how to find food as soon as the fawns can accompany them while they feed, but even after the young start grazing or browsing, there is often a period of overlap when they continue to nurse. Members of small species may be fully weaned as early as two to three months of age. In larger species, the young nurse longer. Red deer fawns may not be fully weaned until they are seven months old.

Deer are considered fawns until they are a year old, at which time they become yearlings. After their second year they are called does, cows, or hinds if they are female. If they are male they are known as bucks, bulls, or stags. Depending on the species, however, they may or may not have reached their full adult size and sexual maturity by that time. Some deer do not mate until they are four or five years old.

The death rate among fawns and yearlings is high. They are killed by predators, exposure, disease, or loss of maternal care if their mothers are killed or abandon them. Researchers have estimated that 30 to 40 percent of white-tailed deer, 50 to 60 percent of fallow deer, and 50 to 70 percent of elk die during their first or second year. Yearling males of territorial species face an additional challenge when they are forced to leave their mothers. Unlike yearling males of social species, they cannot simply join a male herd; they must find a territory they can call their own. If all the nearby territories are already claimed by adult males, a yearling must set off in search of an unclaimed patch. He may have to travel a considerable distance, through unfamiliar territory where he does not know the trails or feeding areas. Mortality for yearling males of territorial species, such as roe deer, muntjac, and pudu, may reach 90 percent. Females have an easier job finding territories, partly because their territories are generally smaller than those of males, and partly because young females often remain in or near their mothers' territories.

Adulthood

A cervid's challenges do not end when it has survived adolescence and managed to establish its own territory or become integrated into a herd. Deer must be constantly alert to the threat of predation. Their enemies in the animal kingdom are many and varied. Depending upon the species of deer and its range, deer are devoured by wolves, bears, mountain lions, tigers, leopards, lynxes, wolverines, badgers, dogs, foxes, and

A YOUNG TIMBER WOLF AND A YOUNG BULL MOOSE FACE OFF IN AN ALASKAN RIVER. IF THE WOLF'S PACK MATES ARE CLOSE AND READY TO HELP, THE MOOSE MAY FIND HIMSELF IN TROUBLE.

wild pigs. Small deer that live in tropical forests are preyed on by large constrictor snakes: pythons in Asia and anacondas in South America.

Predators that actively chase their prey, such as wolves and coyotes, prefer to attack weak prey, which is why fawns are more vulnerable than adults. An adult deer that is sick, exhausted, underfed, or simply slow and unlucky also risks being brought down by these predators. But other predators, including mountain lions and tigers, follow a sit-and-wait strategy, waiting for prey to pass nearby and then leaping out for the ambush. These predators take whatever comes along, including healthy adult deer.

Like all creatures, deer also fall victim to parasites and diseases. Deer species are very vulnerable to a number of diseases, including hemorrhagic fever, blue tongue, and tuberculosis. Just as humans do, deer acquire some degree of immunity to diseases to which they have been exposed for years. Occasionally, though, new illnesses arise, or old ones appear in new places, causing rates of sickness and disease mortality to rise sharply. Currently in the United States, two such conditions are taking a toll on deer populations.

Brainworm is as unpleasant as it sounds. It is an infestation by a parasitic worm called *Parelaphostrongylus tenuis*. It is carried by white-tailed deer, but they are not the sufferers—they have developed immunity. The problem occurs when whitetails pass the parasite to other species. Whitetail dung may contain the brainworm larvae. Snails and slugs that eat the dung become infected with the larvae. Then, when the snails and slugs move on to eat plants, they may be consumed by deer along with the vegetation. In this way the brainworm larvae can enter the digestive systems of deer that are not immune to it, such as moose, elk, and mule deer. When this happens, the larvae bore through the wall of the abomasum and enter the bloodstream. Eventually the worms colonize the spinal column and the brain. First the deer lose the ability to control their bodies, and then they die.

As white-tailed deer extend their range into the American West, sharing habitat and sometimes interbreeding with mule deer, brainworm is becoming more common in mulies. Scientists think that brainworm is also keeping moose from expanding their range southward into parts of North America where the whitetail population is high. The whitetails harbor the brainworm, which makes those areas inhospitable to moose.

The other American deer crisis started in the West. In 1967 wildlife researchers identified a new disease in Colorado mule deer. It is a form of a condition called transmissible spongiform encephalopathy (TSE). Many types of TSE are known to occur in a variety of mammals, and not all of them are fatal. The particular TSE that is attacking deer, though, is always fatal. It is called chronic wasting disease (CWD) because of its effect on deer—they lose weight and simply waste away, becoming slow, listless, and disoriented. Eventually they die. Researchers know that CWD is similar to bovine spongiform encephalopathy, or mad cow disease, and that it passes from one deer to another, but it is not yet known whether CWD can migrate to species beyond deer. In addition to mule deer, whitetails, elk, and moose have been affected by CWD, which has occurred in both wild populations and commercially raised herds. As of 2007, CWD had been documented in thirteen states and two Canadian provinces. There is no known cure or vaccination. The only treatment is to isolate and destroy infected animals.

How long do deer live? For many species, scientists do not have enough information to be sure. Much of the data about deer longevity comes from captive animals, which typically live longer than wild ones, or from records of a few wild specimens that have been tagged and tracked. Some species, however, are better known. The average lifespan of a white-tailed deer in the wild is about ten years. Under ideal conditions, wild muntjac may live for fourteen years, roe deer for sixteen or seventeen, and red deer for more than twenty. A common reason for a deer's death is that the animal's teeth simply wear down over time, and it can no longer eat enough to stay healthy. Weakened by lack of nutrition, an old deer gets sick, falls to predators, or dies of exposure.

5 People and Deer

Three brothers were exploring the countryside in southern France one day in 1910 when they found the entrance to a cave that is now called Trois-Frères ("three brothers") in their honor. Like a number of other caves in France and Spain, Trois-Frères is adorned with wall paintings made by our prehistoric ancestors. Its paintings date from about 13,000 B.C.E. One of them is a striking image of a figure that is part man, part deer. On his head he wears the spreading horns of a stag.

The figure from the cave wall at Trois-Frère is usually called the Sorcerer, but that is just a guess. Although many scholars believe that the figure represents a shaman or mystical warrior, no one knows what importance the painting had for the ancient people who created and viewed it. One thing is clear, though. Deer had value and meaning to those people.

Even without the help of the Sorcerer, archaeologists would know that deer played a vital role in the lives of prehistoric people, as they still do in some traditional cultures today. Bones and other remains found at Stone Age sites show that people ate

IN A HONG KONG MEDICINE SHOP, A RED DEER'S ANTLER IS PREPARED TO BE USED IN FOLK MEDICINES, SUCH AS A SOUP THAT IS BELIEVED TO HELP PEOPLE LIVE LONGER.

deer meat, wore deer skins, and fashioned needles, tools, flutes, and weapon points from deer antlers and bones. The association between humans and deer is an ancient one.

Lore and Literature

Deer appear in the myths and legends of many cultures. In Chinese mythology deer are the companions of the god of longevity, or long life. For this reason the animals are associated with long life and energy. Many traditional Chinese folk medicines call for materials from deer, including ground velvet, powdered antler, or dried and powdered organs. Such remedies are still being produced today, sometimes from animals specifically raised for that purpose but often from wild animals. Because native species of Chinese deer are becoming rare, China imports deer parts from many parts of the world for its folk medicine market.

Artworks found in the tombs of the Scythians, a nomadic people of southern Russia and Ukraine, contain many images of stags with immense branching antlers. Around the same time, the ancient Greeks regarded deer as symbols of Artemis, the goddess of the hunt. In the story of Hercules, one of the hero's labors was capturing a golden-horned hind that belonged to the goddess. Later, the folktales of the Slavic people of southern Russia and the Balkan peninsula featured references to a magical deer with golden horns.

In the literature of the European Renaissance, does and hinds often represented women, the goal of the huntsman's quest. An Italian poet called Petrarch and an English poet named Sir Thomas Wyatt both wrote about a woman who must remain out of reach, using the symbol of a beautiful hind that cannot be hunted because she belongs to the king. Without a doubt, however, the best-known piece of literature about a deer—or at least the best-known movie based on a book about a deer—is the story of Bambi, a young deer. Bambi's tale was told quite differently by the writer and the moviemaker. In both forms, however, it presented a dramatic and influential view of nature and hunting.

Bambi: A Life in the Woods was published in 1926. Its author, an Austrian writer named Felix Salten, was a hunter who owned his own game preserve but became a fervent animal lover and antihunting crusader. *Bambi* told the story of a young deer who witnesses death and destruction being spread through the forest by a powerful, violent, and cruel enemy whom the animals call "Him." That enemy is mankind, who forces all of the natural world to submit to his will. The book is filled with wrenching scenes in which animals either die or are terrorized by the fear of death at human hands. At the end of the book, Bambi's father leads the young deer to the body of a murdered poacher, or illegal hunter. Bambi then realizes that man is not a god or a demon—he is an animal, and he dies like other animals.

Salten's book was widely praised, especially by people who opposed sport hunting. One of those people was an artist named Walt Disney, who in the late 1930s decided to film *Bambi*. The first version of the movie script was fairly faithful to the dark tone of Salten's book. Its animal characters frequently expressed their anguish and their fear and hatred of the cruel humans. Later versions of the script sweetened the tone considerably, adding humor, removing all but one of the direct references to humans, and adding a note of hope and renewed life at the end. Still, when the movie was released in 1942, it caused a sensation. The combination of the finest animated artwork anyone had ever seen with a story of fear and loss gave the movie a powerful emotional impact that sent children—and

THE YOUNG FAWN MEETS FELLOW DWELLERS IN THE FOREST IN THE WALT DISNEY FILM *BAMBI*, BASED ON A BOOK THAT WAS HIGHLY CRITICAL OF HUMAN CRUELTY TO ANIMALS.

many adults—weeping from theaters. Although the movie was less bitter and cynical about humanity than Salten's novel, it took an unmistakably pro-animal, antihunting stand.

Bambi kicked off an argument that continues today. Is it a sentimental, unrealistic, and emotionally manipulative piece of antihunting propaganda? Or is it a work of visionary imagination, a passionate plea for empathy with wild creatures, and a call for ending a cruel and unnecessary practice? Perhaps it is both. Human interactions with deer can be interpreted in a number of ways.

Some hunters blame "the Bambi syndrome" for turning whole generations of young people against hunting. It is true that the number of Americans who hunt is declining. In 1982 about 17 million hunting licenses were issued in the United States. By 2004 that number had dropped to 15 million, although the total population of the country had increased by about 70 million. Among the reasons for the change are the rising cost of hunting licenses and equipment; the loss of hunting grounds to development; the closure of much privately owned land to hunting; the spread of the animal-rights movement; and the appearance of new pastimes, such as videogames.

"Hunting in America has entered a long twilight," declared hunter Steve Tuttle in a 2006 magazine article. The total number of hunters in the United States fell by 7 percent between 1991 and 2001, reports the U.S. Fish and Wildlife Service (FWS). But although hunting seems to be on the decline overall, deer hunting remains by far the most popular kind of hunting in the country. The FWS reported 10.3 million deer hunters in 2001, more than four times as many as for the second most-hunted wild game, turkey. That year eight of every ten American hunters went hunting deer. The number of annual deer licenses issued has increased since the 1990s in some states, while it has fallen in others, in part due to concern about hunting deer infected with chronic wasting disease (CWD).

Hunting for deer, elk, and moose is not going to disappear. It remains a deeply pleasurable and meaningful part of life for many outdoorspeople in the United States and other parts of the world. Deer hunting also has a big economic impact. In addition to providing food for many hunters and their families, deer hunting produces income for the companies that manufacture hunting gear, the communities that sell services to hunters, and the local and state governments that collect money from the sale of hunting licenses. In 2001 American deer hunters spent an estimated $10.7 billion on their sport.

When deer hunting is done legally, regulated by state and federal wildlife agencies, it plays an important role in wildlife management. The officials who oversee national parks and other public lands, as well as those charged with maintaining and controlling populations of wild animals, decide how many deer hunters can harvest each year—and they also count on hunters to keep the number of deer within limits, so that the animals do not become too numerous for the available food and habitat. Hunting is one piece of the overall strategy of managing deer populations.

Managing and Conserving Deer

As of 2007, no deer species is endangered in the United States. However, two subspecies of white-tailed deer—the Columbian white-tailed deer of the Pacific Northwest and the Key deer of the Florida Keys—have been identified are endangered. Neither of them is currently hunted. Moose, elk, caribou, and deer are among the most studied and managed species on publicly owned land, such as national forest and Bureau of Land Management property. Government wildlife agencies consider it important to safeguard those species, partly because of their value as game animals. The money raised by selling hunting licenses and fees is an important part of conservation funding.

In Europe, species that are valued as game animals, such as red deer and fallow deer, are monitored and offered some protected habitat. By and large, the European species of deer are in good shape. Elsewhere in the world, though, the picture is less bright for deer. The World Conservation Union (IUCN), an

AN OREGON WILDLIFE BIOLOGIST RECORDS INFORMATION ABOUT A NEWBORN
ELK CALF. THE CALF WILL BE FITTED WITH A RADIO COLLAR THAT WILL HELP
SCIENTISTS MONITOR ITS MOVEMENTS AND HEALTH. THROUGH THOUSANDS OF SUCH
RESEARCH PROJECTS AROUND THE WORLD, PEOPLE ARE NOT JUST STUDYING DEER BUT
ACTIVELY MANAGING THEM AND, IN MANY CASES, WORKING TO PROTECT SPECIES THAT
ARE AT RISK.

international association of conservation groups, releases an
annual survey of plant and animals species that are endangered,
threatened, or at risk of becoming threatened. In 2006 this Red
List, as it is called, identified thirteen species of Asian and South
American cervids as endangered, vulnerable, or near threatened. Among them were two species of axis deer, the tufted
deer, the pampas deer, the Calamian and Bawaen deer, the
pudus, Chinese water deer, the marsh deer, the Philippine

spotted deer, and the black muntjac. One species of *Cervus*, Schomburgk's deer, was identified as extinct; it was last seen in Thailand in 1932. The 2006 Red List also identified four of the five species of musk deer as vulnerable or near threatened. The biggest immediate threats to the survival of all of these at-risk species are human-caused habitat loss and overhunting.

Conservation measures take several forms. One approach is to protect some animals in zoos or small preserves where they can be guarded against poaching. Even if the deer's habitat is lost, the species will survive. This last-ditch approach may be needed to save the rarest species from extinction, but many deer fail to thrive in captivity. A better method is to preserve enough safe habitat for the species to live in the wild, but this can be extremely difficult, especially with species such as the pudu and musk deer that live in remote regions of developing nations, where there is little money or motivation to safeguard them. In parts of Asia and South America, international wildlife agencies are working to establish preserves, parks, and migration corridors that would ensure adequate, safe habitat for deer along with many other species, but it is sometimes an uphill struggle.

Managing and conserving even healthy populations of deer is not easy, as American wildlife managers have learned. The white-tailed deer is an example of how human activities can quickly bring about big changes in deer populations, sometimes with unforeseen results. Biologists estimate that at the beginning of the nineteenth century there were about 40 million whitetails in the United States. Over the course of the century they were very heavily hunted and sometimes simply exterminated as pests that destroyed crops; they also suffered the loss of much forest habitat. By the 1920s, whitetails had disappeared from many parts of their former range, and their total population was believed to have fallen below half a million. Hunting regulations were put into place during the 1930s, and wildlife preserves were established or expanded to protect the deer. Groups of whitetails were reintroduced into selected spots in their former ranges. Wildlife managers hoped that the species would recover.

It did. The reintroductions and other measures were so successful that by the beginning of the twenty-first century estimates of the whitetail population ranged as high as 30 million. Not only had the deer reestablished themselves throughout their former range, they had even moved west into areas where they were formerly unknown, or rare.

During the same decades that the white-tailed deer was bouncing back, however, the human population of the country was also rising. The second half of the twentieth century saw significant increases in suburban housing, road building, and traffic. These trends put people on a collision course with deer—literally. According to Michael Conover, author of *Resolving Human-Animal Conflicts: The Science of Wildlife Damage Management* (2001), more than 1.4 million deer are killed by cars or trucks each year in the United States alone. These collisions take a human toll, too. In the United States they kill about 200 people each year, injure some 29,000 people, and cause an estimated $1.6 billion of damage to automobiles. In another unwelcome development, whitetails have become so numerous in some agricultural and residential areas that they have become destructive pests.

When regulated hunting fails to keep deer populations under control, wildlife managers may turn to culling, which is the controlled killing of a certain percentage of the population, to keep deer numbers manageable. In the early part of the twentieth century, big carnivores such as bears, wolves, and mountain lions were exterminated throughout much of the American West. Wolves, the chief predator of deer, were eliminated with special thoroughness because they also preyed on livestock. With the top predators out of the way, mule deer populations soared, rapidly outgrowing the available food sources. With thousands of mule deer dead or starving and mortality rates for fawns skyrocketing, wildlife managers finally chose to cull the herds aggressively. The slaughter of deer led to a public outcry, and slowly the general public began to learn what many biologists and wildlife managers had already discovered: achieving and maintaining an acceptable population level for deer through active management is extremely difficult.

The deer of New Zealand illustrate another wildlife management dilemma—the introduced species. Humans love some types of deer so much that they have transplanted them all around the world. Red deer, sika deer, wapiti, fallow deer, and whitetails have each been introduced to the Pacific island nation of New Zealand, where they have no natural predators or competitors. The deer flourished in their new home, feasting on vegetation that had been the food and natural habitat of New Zealand's birds, trampling meadows and forests that had never known the hooves of ungulates, and becoming a serious pest problem for the country's farmers and sheep ranchers.

Since the 1930s the government of New Zealand has employed one culling scheme after another, including using helicopters to hunt deer in remote mountain regions. Surveys in the 1980s and 1990s suggested that the number of red deer, at least, was falling. Short of exterminating all deer—which would probably not be possible, even if it were acceptable to the public—the country has no choice but to consider deer a new and somewhat troublesome member of its fauna, or animal population. At the same time, ironically, farming deer for venison (deer meat) and antler velvet is becoming big business in New Zealand.

Deer and people have been linked for a long, long time, as the stag-horned Sorcerer on the wall at Trois-Frères reminds us. The challenge that faces us now is to save the rare and endangered species of deer, and to wisely manage those that are thriving, so that deer continue to be part of our world in the future.

Glossary

adapt—change or develop in ways that aid survival in the environment

ancestral—having to do with lines of descent or earlier forms

artiodactyl—an ungulate with two hoofed toes on each foot, sometimes called a cloven-hoofed animal (includes pigs, cattle, goats, camels, and other ungulates in addition to deer)

browse—to eat coarse or woody vegetation that is found off the ground, such as leaves, twigs, bark, and shoots

buck—male deer (except moose, elk, caribou, and red deer); most often used in the United States to refer to male white-tailed and mule deer

bull—male moose, elk, or caribou

cervid—a deer; relating to deer

conservation—action or movement aimed at preserving wildlife or its habitat

doe—female deer, except moose, elk, and caribou, which are called cows

estrus—mating period of a female mammal; phase of the reproductive cycle in which the animal may become pregnant

evolve—to change over time; evolution is the pattern of new species, or types of plants and animals, emerging from old ones

extinct—no longer existing, died out

fawn—deer in the first year of life, except young moose, elk, and caribou, which are called calves

graze—to eat grass or other easily digested vegetation that grows on the ground

habitat—type of environment in which an animal lives

hind—female red deer

longevity—length of life; often refers to long lives

metabolism—chemical processes by which an animal uses energy and maintains or builds tissue

paleontologist—scientist who practices paleontology, the study of ancient and extinct life forms, usually by examining fossil remains

pedicle—bony growth on a deer's skull from which an antler grows

rumination—a process of digestion that involves regurgitating and rechewing food to prepare it for digestion by microorganisms in a multipart stomach; ungulates that digest their food this way are called ruminants

saltation or **saltatorial running**—a rapid gait in which the animal bounds strongly upward and forward

sexual dimorphism—difference in physical form between males and females of a species; most deer species are sexually dimorphic, with males larger than females, and bearing horns

stag—male red deer

stotting—a type of bounding or bouncing locomotion in which all four of a deer's feet leave the ground at the same time

tine—prong growing out of the main branch of an antler

ungulate—hoofed mammal

SPECIES CHECKLIST

A number of different taxonomies, or systems of classification, exist for deer. The species on this list are accepted by many scientists. Some classifications, however, recognize more species than are shown here, while others recognize fewer.

Family Moschidae (Musk Deer)

	Himalayan musk deer	*Moschus chrysogaster*
	Nepal musk deer	*Moschus leucogaster*
	Chinese or black musk deer	*Moschus fuscus*
	Forest musk deer	*Moschus berezovski*
	Siberian musk deer	*Moschus moschiferus*

Family Cervidae (Deer)

Subfamily Hydropotinae	Chinese water deer	*Hydropotes inermis*
Subfamily Cervulinae or Muntiacinae	Indian muntjac	*Muntiacus muntjak*
	Borneo muntjac	*Muntiacus atherodes*
	Reeve's muntjac	*Muntiacus reevesi*
	Fea's muntjac	*Muntiacus feae*
	Tibetan muntjac	*Muntiacus gongshanensis*
	Black muntjac	*Muntiacus crinifrons*
	Giant muntjac	*Muntiacus vuquangensis*
	Leaf deer or leaf muntjac	*Muntiacus putaoensis*
	Tufted deer	*Elaphodus cephalophus*
Subfamily Cervinae (Eurasian deer)	White-lipped or Thorold's deer	*Cervus albirostris*
	Barasingha or swamp deer	*Cervus duvauceli*
	Red Deer	*Cervus elaphus*
	Wapiti or American elk	*Cervus canadensis*
	Thamin or Eld's deer	*Cervus eldii*
	Philippine sambar or brown deer	*Cervus mariannus*
	Sika	*Cervus nippon*
	Sunda sambar or rusa	*Cervus timorensis*
	Schomburgk's deer*	*Cervus Schomburgki*
	Calamian deer	*Axis calamiansis*

	Bawean or Kuhl's deer	*Axis kuhlii*
	Hog deer	*Axis porcinus*
	Père David's deer	*Elaphurus davidianus*
	Fallow deer	*Dama dama*
	Persian fallow deer	*Dama mesopotamica*
Subfamily Odocoileinae or Capreolinae (American deer)	Caribou or reindeer	*Rangifer tarandus*
	Moose or European elk	*Alces alces*
	Roe deer	*Capreolus capreolus*
	Mule or black-tailed deer	*Odocoileus hemionus*
	White-tailed deer	*Odocoileus virginianus*
	Pampas deer	*Ozotoceros bezoarcticus*
	Red brocket	*Mazama americana*
	Dwarf brocket	*Mazama chunyi*
	Brown brocket	*Mazama gouazoubira*
	Yucatan brown brocket	*Mazama pandora*
	Little red brocket	*Mazama rufina*
	Northern pudu	*Pudu mephistophiles*
	Southern pudu	*Pudu pudu*
	Marsh deer	*Blastocerus dichotomus*
	Peruvian huemul or North Andean deer	*Hippocamelus antisensis*
	Chilean huemul or South Andean deer	*Hippocameula bisulcus*

*Probably extinct.

Further Research

Books for Young People

Blair, Diane and Pamela Wright. *Deer Watching*. Mankato, MN: Capstone. 2000.

DuTemple, Lesley A. *North American Moose*. Minneapolis, MN: Carolrhoda, 2001.

Frahm, Randy. *Deer Hunting*. Mankato, MN: Capstone, 2001.

Jacobs, Lee. *Deer*. San Diego, CA: Blackbirch, 2002.

Sullivan, Jody. *Deer: Graceful Grazers*. Mankato, MN: Capstone, 2003.

Videos and DVDs

Being Caribou. National Film Board of Canada, n.d.

Florida's Key Deer. International Video Projects, 2004.

Living Edens: Denali—Alaska's Great Wilderness. PBS Home Video, 1997.

Majestic Whitetails. Westlake Entertainment, 2003.

Web Sites

Some useful Web sites about deer are listed here. Since this book was written, some of these sites may have changed, moved to new addresses, or gone out of existence. New sites may now be available. In addition to these Web sites, many others also provide information about deer.

http://animaldiversity.ummz.umich.edu/site/accounts/information/Cervidae.html

> This site about the family Cervidae (deer) is part of the Animal Diversity Web (ADW) of the University of Michigan Museum of Zoology; the ADW also has sites on related families such as the musk deer and mouse deer.

http://www.worlddeer.org/index.html

> Created with the help of Germany's Siegen University, the World Deer site offers a good overview of deer classification as well as information on deer biology and conservation.

http://www.ultimateungulate.com/

> Zoologist Brent Huffman is the author of The Ultimate Ungulate, an Internet resource for information about all of the world's hoofed mammals, including all branches of the deer family tree. His classification scheme recognizes more deer species than many other classifications do.

http://www.nhptv.org/natureworks/moose.htm

http://www.nhptv.org/Natureworks/whitetaileddeer.htm

> New Hampshire Public Television maintains these pages on the white-tailed deer and the moose.

http://www.adfg.state.ak.us/pubs/notebook/biggame/moose.php

http://www.adfg.state.ak.us/pubs/notebook/biggame/caribou.php

> These pages of information on moose and caribou are part of the Wildlife Notebook Series of the Alaska Department of Fish and Game.

Bibliography

Cartmill, Matt. "The Bambi Syndrome." *Natural History*, June 1993, Vol. 102, Issue 6, p. 6.

Clutton-Brock, Tim. "Lords of the Lek," *Natural History*, October 1991, Vol. 100, Issue 10, p. 34.

Conover, Michael. *Resolving Human-Animal Conflict: The Science of Wildlife Damage Management*. Boca Raton, FL: CRC, 2001.

Diamond, Jared. "Must We Shoot Deer to Save Nature?" *Natural History*, August 1992, Vol. 101, Issue 8, p. 2.

Geist, Valerius. *Deer of the World: Their Evolution, Behaviour, and Ecology*. Mechanicsburg, PA: Stackpole Books, 1998.

Gould, Stephen Jay. "The Misnamed, Mistreated, and Misunderstood Irish Elk." *Ever Since Darwin*. New York: Norton, 1977.

Heffelfinger, Jim. *Deer of the Southwest*. College Station, TX: Texas A & M University, 2006.

Putman, Rory. *The Natural History of Deer*. Ithaca, NY: Comstock, 1988.

Rue, Leonard Lee. *The Encyclopedia of Deer*. Stillwater, MN: Voyageur, 2003.

Smith, Doug. "The Mystery of the Disappearing Moose," *National Wildlife*, February/March 2007, Vol. 45, Issue 2.

Tuttle, Steve. "The Elusive Hunter." *Newsweek*, December 4, 2006, online at http://www.msnbc.msn.com/id/15892909/site/newsweek/page/1

Whitehead, G. Kenneth. *Deer of the World*. New York: Viking, 1972.

Index

Page numbers in **boldface** are illustrations.

About the Author

Rebecca Stefoff has written numerous nonfiction books for readers of all ages. Among her books on scientific topics are several other volumes in the AnimalWays series, including *Horses, Tigers,* and *Chimpanzees.* Stefoff has also written for Benchmark Books' Family Trees series, which explores the relationships among different groups of living things. She is the author of *Charles Darwin and the Evolution Revolution* (Oxford, 1996) and appeared in the A&E *Biography* episode on Darwin and his work. Find out more about the author and her books at www.rebeccastefoff.com.